BALKRISHNA M. SADEKAR i
Candlestick Charting LLC., an
training to stock traders in the proper use of candlestick charting
and technical analysis. He is also a member of Technical
Securities Analyst Association (TSAASF.org), a leading
authority for technical analysis in the United States.

With a Masters degree in Engineering, Sadekar has passionately
blended technology with investor psychology analysis *via*
candlestick charts. A trader for more than a decade, he has
trained and continues training novice and experienced traders in
correctly applying trading systems for profiting from equity
markets.

Sadekar resides in Richmond, VA in the US and can be reached
via his website, www.ProfitableCandlestickCharting.com. His
first book, *How to Make Money with Candlestick Charts*, also
published by Vision Books, is a bestseller.

HOW TO MAKE MONEY TRADING THE ICHIMOKU SYSTEM Guide to Candlestick Cloud Charts

Balkrishna M. Sadekar

VISION
BOOKS

www.visionbooksindia.com

www.visionbooksindia.com

First Published 2016
Reprinted 2017 (Twice)

A Vision Books Original

ISBN 10: 81-7094-955-6
ISBN 13: 978-81-7094-955-8

Published by
Vision Books Pvt. Ltd.
(Incorporating Orient Paperbacks & CARING imprints)
24 Feroze Gandhi Road, Lajpat Nagar 3
New Delhi-110024, India
Phone: (+91-11) 2984 0821 / 22
email: visionbooks@gmail.com

Printed at
Anand Sons
C 88, Ganesh Nagar, Pandav Nagar Complex
Delhi 110 092, India.

Contents

Acknowledgements

I would like to thank my loving parents and in-laws for their support throughout my life. I am also grateful for the wonderful support and love from my sister and her family.

I would like to thank folks at Chart Nexus for allowing me use of their stock charts. They have created an excellent technical analysis charting platform with all the necessary tools needed for evaluating stock charts.

I am thankful again to Vision Books India for believing in my efforts and publishing my second book with them.

Lastly, a special thanks to the two amazing individuals in my life, my wife and daughter. They continue to push me to achieve the best.

1

Introduction

Ichimoku Kinko Hyu, commonly referred to as Ichimoku, is one of the best systems available for trading the markets. The Ichimoku indicator can be applied to stocks, commodities, futures, currencies and bonds. If you can chart it, you can apply Ichimoku to it. It works very well on all time frames, from the weekly all the way down to one minute chart. For those familiar with candlestick charts, Ichimoku charts are a default extension of Japanese innovation.

Loosely translated, Ichimoku chart means a 'one glance equilibrium' chart. **Once a trader is familiar with the components of an Ichimoku system, it should take no more than a glance to decide if the chart is bullish or bearish.** This was the purpose with which Goichi Hosoda invented this system. Goichi was a Japanese reporter who wanted to create an all-in-one indicator to visually depict the market's sentiment in the chart. After fine tuning it for many years, he finally published his findings in Japan in the late 1960s. This was the first publication on Ichimoku system and it got rapidly adopted by the Japanese traders and across Asia. Ichimoku started getting a following in the Western world in the 1990s as computers became widespread. The computation involved in developing and displaying the indicator got a lot easier with the help of computers. Most charting platforms today offer Ichimoku as an indicator.

The Important Numbers

The Ichimoku system is based on three numbers: 9, 26 and 52.

There are a few theories about why these numbers were used by Goichi when he developed the system.

In Japan, there were 26 trading days in a month in those days. So 52 days would account for two months of trading activity. The number 9 was about a week-and-a-half of trading. Another theory proposes that the number 26 was based on a lunar cycle. The fact is that it really does not matter. The Ichimoku system works with amazing accuracy with these original numbers. Traders often try to change and experiment with the number settings. There's nothing wrong with that and you might want to do so as well. Please make sure, however, that you are not curve-fitting the settings. You might find some settings working flawlessly on a 5-minute chart, but when you try to use them on the daily chart, they fail dramatically. So keep that in mind if you want to play with different numbers on your Ichimoku chart. **I would strongly suggest using the original numbers as they have stood the test of time on all time frames and across all asset classes.**

As mentioned earlier, Ichimoku charts are meant to show investor sentiment at a glance. Another huge advantage of this system is that there is no need for other indicators and oscillators. One of the big dilemmas traders face is what indicators or oscillators to use. Choosing between hundreds of them and experimenting with their individual settings is a daunting task. Most times traders will use an indicator for a few trades and if the trades don't work, move on to the next indicator. This way, they never really get to experience the indicator in all situations. They keep moving from indicator to indicator and from one trading system to another, finally blowing out their account. There is no indicator, oscillator or trading system out there which will work 100% of the time. So is Ichimoku the holy grail for traders? Obviously not! The holy grail in trading is a myth. Each system has its flaws. It is how a trader uses the system that makes the system profitable. Remember that the goal of trading is to make more profits than losses. It is not to make only profitable trades. That is impossible. In fact, research has shown that successful traders have a higher number of losing trades than winning ones. They are successful because of one simple reason. The profits in their profitable trades are far higher than the losses in their losing trades. Most inexperienced traders have exactly the opposite situation. They go for quick profits, but let the losers run. This mindset needs to change! The Ichimoku system, with its dynamic support / resistance components is well suited to help the trader in adhering to strict rules.

Price Equilibrium

The core of the Ichimoku system is built around the relationship between price and its equilibrium. In the Western world, equilibrium is based on closing prices of an asset. An example of this would be a 50- or 200-period simple moving average. Technical analysts will often refer to these as equilibrium for price; namely, the price cannot stray too far from them and has to revert back sooner or later. In the Japanese world, the high and low of the trading period is considered equally important as the price open and close. The high is the point where demand was overwhelmed by supply. The low is where buyers provided enough demand to absorb supply. These two price extremes give the range of trading activity for that period. This range changes every period and is dynamic. If prices do not make new highs and new lows within a certain amount of time, the equilibrium will be maintained and price could gravitate towards it. In bullish trends, this equilibrium keeps moving higher as the price achieves new highs. In bearish markets, on the other hand, the equilibrium moves lower as the lows keep falling. These trends continue so long as the demand / supply relationship doesn't revert. When it does, price breaks out through the equilibrium and starts moving in the opposite direction.

In Ichimoku, equilibrium is calculated as the average of the highest high and the lowest low in three different periods. Any guesses which three periods?

Yes, 9, 26 and 52!

Ichimoku is a Trend Following System

Most successful traders make their money trading trends. It is extremely difficult to derive profits from a non-trending market. Ichimoku helps mitigate this issue to a certain extent. It helps the trader in identifying non-trending markets, so that they can be avoided. As you will read in the next chapter, **the Ichimoku system has a built-in zone, called the Kumo cloud, which signifies consolidation**. Traders need to be extra cautious initiating trades when the price is within the Kumo, as it is then in a non-trending phase.

The individual components of Ichimoku are designed to provide the following information:

- Is the chart bullish or bearish?

- Is the chart displaying consolidation of price?

- If the chart is bullish, is there momentum in the trend?

- If the chart is bearish, is there momentum in the trend?

- If a chart is consolidating, how long would it be before the consolidation might get over?

- Where is the price equilibrium? For bullish markets, this would be support; and for bearish markets this would be resistance.

Future Projection and Past Influence

Another in-built feature of Ichimoku is the projection of future price action. Goichi firmly believed that current price action has repercussions in the future. Demand and supply available in the present will create support and resistance in the future. Based on this assumption, the Ichimoku system is designed to project dynamic support and resistance values 26 periods ahead in time. No other indicator has such a future predicting feature.

Just as the present affects the future, the past also influences the present. Accordingly, prices from 26 periods ago are given great importance in the Ichimoku system. As Chapter 2 describes, traders need to be particularly aware of this phenomenon.

I would urge the reader to read and re-read Chapters 2 and 3 until the Ichimoku components and their significance is clear and well understood. Chapters 4 and 5 constitute a practical guide to Ichimoku trading.

Welcome to the world of Ichimoku! You will profit from it.

2

Ichimoku Components

The Ichimoku system has five components to it:

- Tenkan;

- Kijun;

- Senkou A;

- Senkou B; and

- Chikou.

The Senkou A and Senkou B together form a structure commonly known as the Kumo cloud.

We will explain the five components in this chapter. Keep in mind that these components are highly effective when used as a system. Chapter 3 will deal in detail about integrating the five components together to form a trading system.

Tenkan

Tenkan, also known as 'the Conversion Line,' is calculated by averaging the highest high and the lowest low of the previous 9 periods. Keep in mind that the Japanese place a lot of importance on how the price behaves during the entire trading period. The high and the low of the day are as important as the open and close of the candle on the candlestick chart. The high point of the candle is where demand was overcome by supply and the low point of the candle is where supply was absorbed by the demand. This is the crucial point of candlestick charts and is carried over in the Ichimoku as well. In other words, **the average of the high and low will give the equilibrium of price for that period.** So the average of highest high and lowest low of the last 9 periods will provide an equilibrium point for price over the previous 9 periods.

Tenkan = (Highest high of 9 periods + Lowest low of 9 periods) ÷ 2

Please note that the Tenkan differs from the 9-period exponential moving average (EMA) and the 9-period simple moving average (SMA). Both SMA and EMA are based on closing prices and are much smoother than Tenkan. Tenkan, by its very nature, will exhibit periods of flattening as can be seen in Figure 2.1.

If a stock jumps up and then starts moving sideways without making any new 9-period highs, then the Tenkan will go flat thus visually indicating that price is consolidating. At that point, either the price will come down to the Tenkan to find equilibrium or, after 9 periods, the Tenkan will start to rise to support the price.

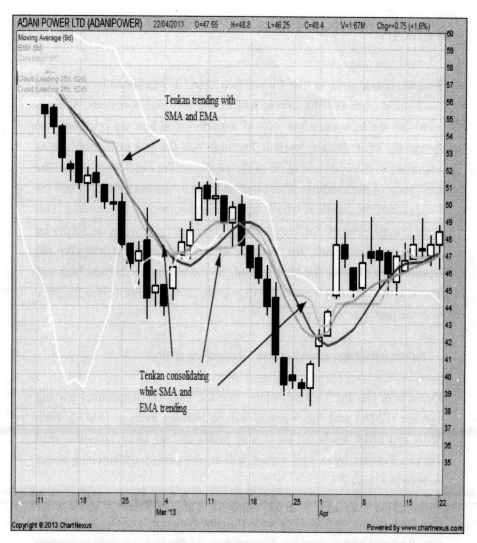

Figure 2.1: **Tenkan *versus* EMA and SMA; notice the flattening of Tenkan in the right hand part of the chart**

One can think of Tenkan as a short term "magnetic" guide for the price. Price cannot stray too far from the equilibrium that Tenkan represents. For stocks in an uptrend, Tenkan acts as a minor support level. On the other hand, for stocks in a downtrend, Tenkan provides minor resistance.

You can see how Tenkan keeps providing support for the price in the chart of Axis Bank in Figure 2.2. Price often times breaks the Tenkan intraday, but closes back above it indicating bulls coming in to defend the equilibrium.

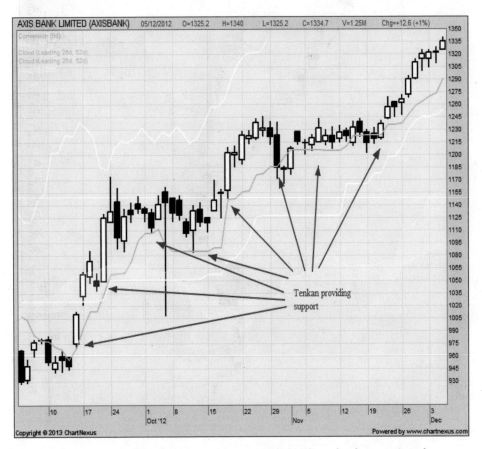

Figure 2.2: **Tenkan provides minor support for the price in an uptrend**

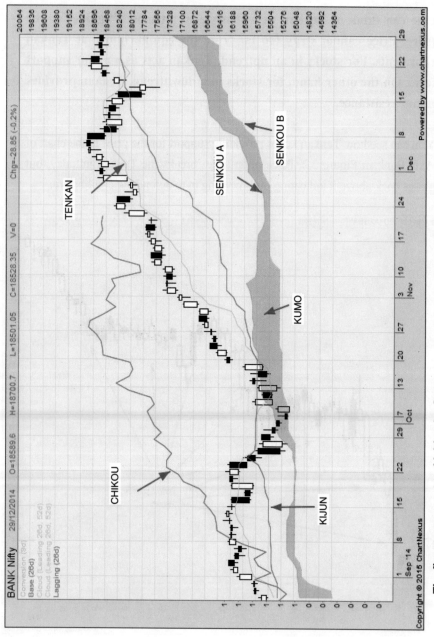

The five components of Ichimoku System — the Tenkan, Kijun, the Kumo made up of Senkou A and Senkou B, and the Chikou

Figure 2.3: **Tenkan provides minor resistance to price in Bajaj Hindustan's downtrend**

Correspondingly, chart of Bajaj Hindustan in Figure 2.3 shows the various times that Tenkan provided resistance to any potential reversal in price.

Kijun

The Kijun, also called the 'Base Line' is primarily a trend container. It is calculated by averaging the highest high and the lowest low of the previous 26 periods. Just like the Tenkan, the period can mean a 1-minute, 5-minute or any other time frame. So the formula for Kijun is as follows:

Kijun = (Highest high of 26 periods + Lowest low of 26 periods) ÷ 2

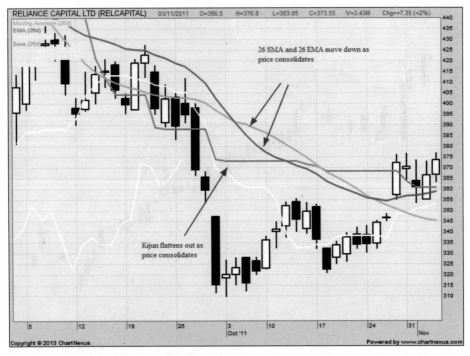

Figure 2.4: **Kijun *versus* EMA and SMA; note how the Kijun is more sensitive to price highs and lows**

Traders should not compare Kijun to a regular 26-period simple moving average or exponential moving average. As the chart in Figure 2.4 shows, the Kijun is more sensitive to price highs and lows and does not care about prices moving within the 26-period high / low areas. In the chart in Figure 2.4, you would notice that while the 26-period SMA and EMA keep moving up, the Kijun goes flat. **The Kijun denotes equilibrium between the buyers and sellers.** If prices over the last 26 periods are fluctuating in a range, the equilibrium will be at the mid-point of this range. This point will attract prices back to it like a magnet. As Figure 2.4 shows, the EMA and SMA are lagging indicators. Even though prices started going lower, these moving averages kept going higher. The Kijun will be horizontal as soon as the stock stops making new highs and consolidates.

- If prices are above the Kijun, it is considered bullish.

- If prices are below the Kijun, it is considered bearish.

Can the price move below the Kijun intra-time period? Sure it can. The key is that it should not close decisively below it. As long as prices close above the Kijun, the stock is considered in an uptrend. Once the price closes below it, the uptrend is considered broken. This does not mean a downtrend has started. As you will see in the later chapters, all the Ichimoku components together alone tell the whole story.

Notice how the Tata Power stock in Figure 2.5 occasionally dipped below the Kijun during the uptrend until it finally broke down and closed below it.

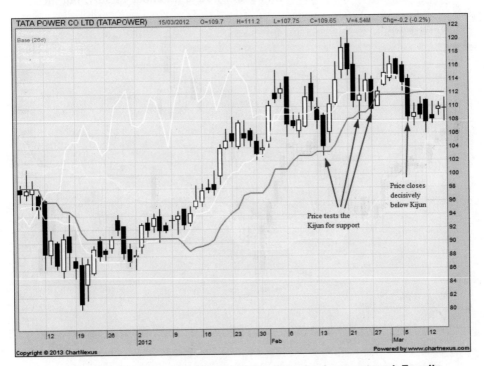

Figure 2.5: **Kijun provides major support to the price in an uptrend. Equally, it provides resistance to the price in a downtrend**

The Kijun provides strong support for the price in an uptrend. It also offers a strong resistance to the price in a downtrend.

Prices cannot get too far away from the Kijun. Again, keep in mind that the Kijun represents equilibrium. Prices need to always be in sync with the equilibrium. That is where demand and supply are balanced. Consider the chart in Figure 2.6 to understand how the Kijun acts as a magnet for prices.

After the downtrend, some event occurs to trigger exuberant buying in the stock. This can be seem in the middle of the chart. This surge in demand leads to an exponential price increase in a short period of time. Prices cannot keep rising that fast for too long, however. This leads to the Kijun initially reacting to the price, from about 27 June till about 11 July, but then

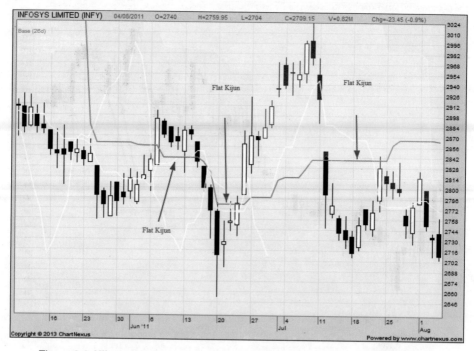

Figure 2.6: **Kijun acting as a magnet for the price, attracting it back to itself time and again when it moves too far away**

going flat as the stock could not make new highs. The flat Kijun now starts attracting the price back to it.

Scenarios of exiting a trade when the price has considerably extended from Kijun, will often lead to losses. They are best avoided for swing trading.

Figure 2.7 shows such a quick move to the upside. Anyone would want to take profits off the table if presented with a 28% gain in a couple of weeks. Now, if enough traders decide to take profits, then guess where the stock is heading? Down to its equilibrium!

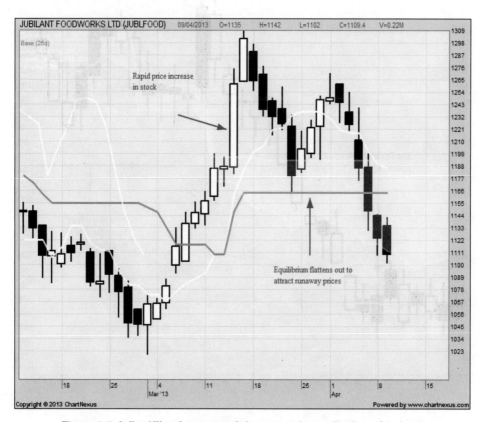

Figure 2.7: **A flat Kijun is a powerful magnet that pulls the price back towards itself**

Ichimoku allows the trader to visually anticipate when the equilibrium is going to shift up or down. Since we know that the Kijun is the average price of the highest high and lowest low of the previous 26 periods, one can notice from the chart if any of those two parameters are due for a change. Study the chart of Axis Bank in Figure 2.8. Can you predict what Kijun will do the next day?

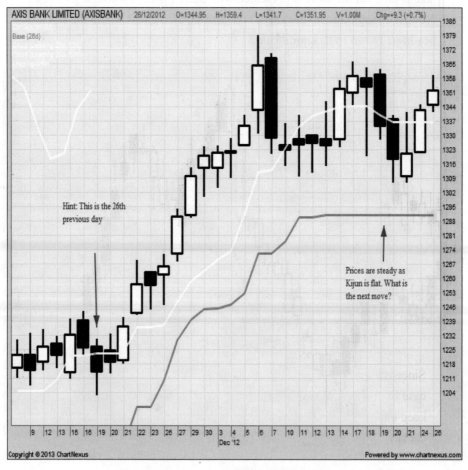

Figure 2.8: **Price consolidation waiting for Kijun**

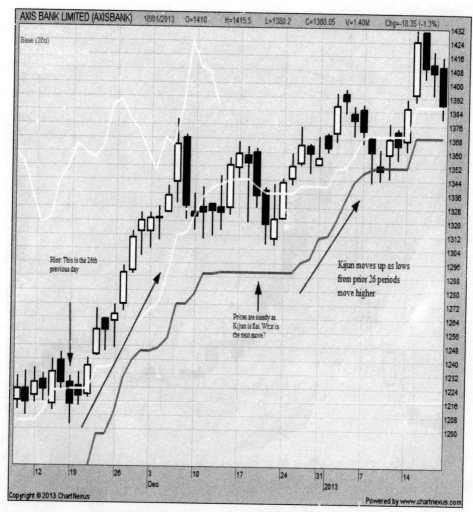

Figure 2.9: **Price breaks out as the Kijun starts trending**

Since the low of 25 days back was higher than the low 26 days ago in the case of Axis Bank (*see* Figure 2.9), the Kijun will move up. As the lows keep getting higher, one can expect the Kijun to trend up nicely to support the stock.

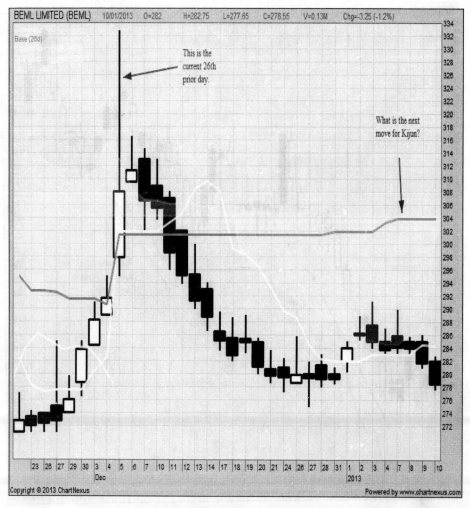

Figure 2.10: **The Flat Kijun will start heading down soon**

The same analysis holds true for a stock in a downtrend. Notice how in Figure 2.10, the Kijun is flat at this point.

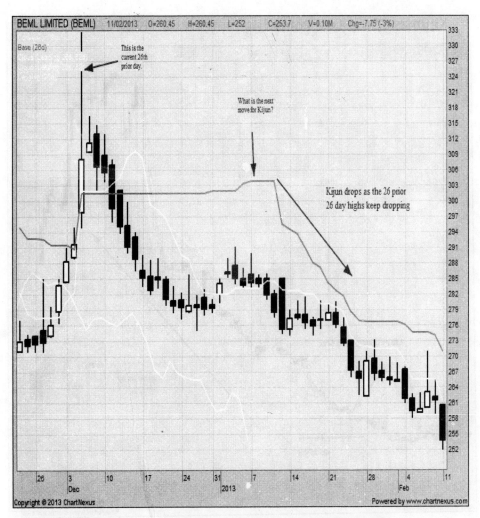

Figure 2.11: **Price heads south as the Kijun trends down**

Now continuing the story from Figure 2.10, the 26-period highs will keep dropping from 5 December. This will turn the Kijun down and it will offer resistance to the stock as can be seen in the chart in Figure 2.11.

Kijun as a Stop Loss Point

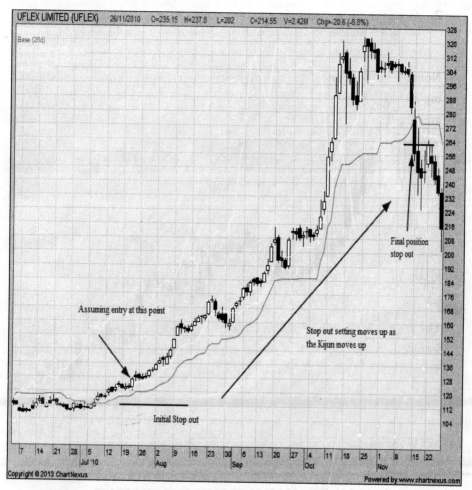

Figure 2.12: **Kijun used as a stop out signal**

The Kijun is often used as the stop loss point in a trade. A small buffer allowing for intraday movement (assuming a daily chart) should be used below the Kijun for setting the stop loss. In an uptrend, as the stock makes new 26-period highs, the Kijun will start moving up. This allows the trader to move up the stop loss setting as well. This helps in two ways.

1. It reduces any potential loss until the trade reaches breakeven.
2. Once the trade reaches breakeven, it allows the trader to lock in more profits as the equilibrium moves up.

Notice how in Figure 2.12, the stop out setting for the stock keeps moving higher allowing the trader to lock in bigger profits as the trade progresses.

There could be an occasional instance when the stock gaps against you and below the stop out level. There is not much a trader can do about that, but to close out the trade and move on to the next one.

Kumo

The Kumo is the heart of the Ichimoku system and is commonly referred to as the cloud. It is made up of two individual components, the Senkou A and Senkou B. We will first look at each of these components and then discuss their aggregation into the Kumo cloud.

Senkou A

Now that you are familiar with the Tenkan and Kijun, it is easy to understand the Senkou A, also referred to as 'Span A.'

Senkou A is the average of the two components, namely Tenkan and Kijun, and is projected 26 days in the future on the chart.

Senkou A = (Tenkan + Kijun) ÷ 2

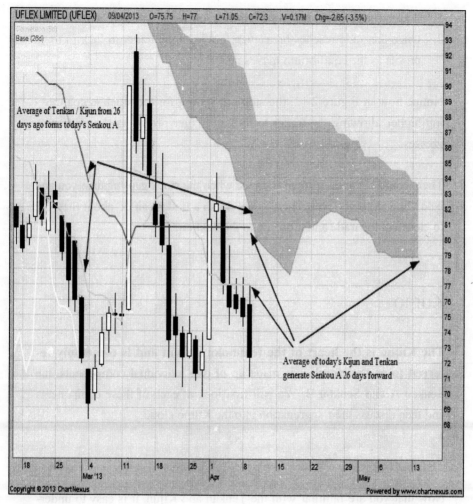

Figure 2.13: **Senkou A — and its relationship with Tenkan and Kijun**

Figure 2.13 shows the relationship between Tenkan, Kijun and Senkou A.

To make it clearer, today's Senkou A would be formed by averaging the Tenkan and Kijun values of 26 days ago. On the same note, today's Tenkan and Kijun values, when averaged, will create the Senkou A point 26 days in the future.

If the Senkou A (26 days in the future) is rising, it is considered bullish for the stock.

If it is declining, then the stock would be considered to be in a bearish mode.

The current Senkou A can provide support for a rising stock (*see* Figure 2.14).

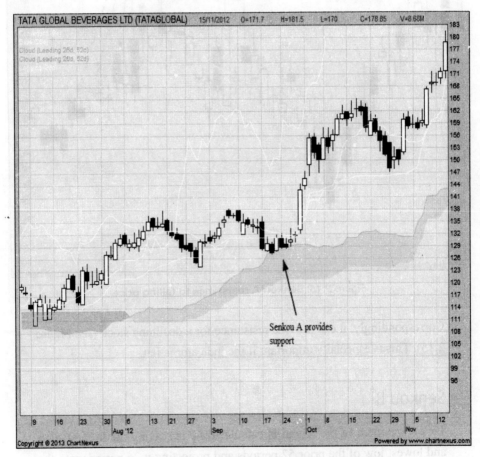

Figure 2.14: **Senkou A providing support to rising price**

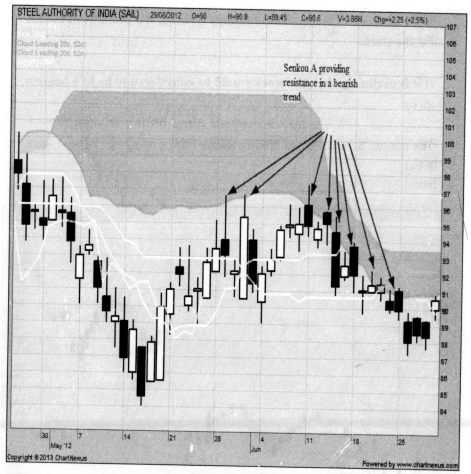

Figure 2.15: **Senkou A resistance to falling price**

Correspondingly, it can provide resistance for a declining stock (*see* Figure 2.15). This is especially important if the indicator is flat.

Senkou B

This component of the Kumo is calculated by averaging the highest high and lowest low of the prior 52 periods and projecting it 26 periods into the future. It is essentially the equilibrium for prices over the past 52 periods, plotted 26 days in the future on the chart.

Senkou B = (Highest high of prior 52 periods + Lowest low of prior 52 periods) ÷ 2

Again, to make it clearer, today's Senkou B value was formed 26 days back. The value that one sees on the chart in Figure 2.16, 26 days in the future was arrived at by averaging the highest high and the lowest low period by the price over the past 52 periods, starting from today.

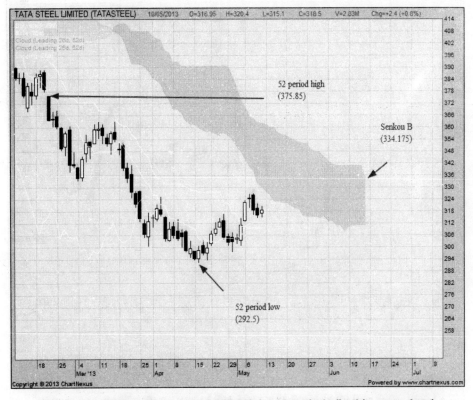

Figure 2.16: **Senkou B's value of 334.175 for 26 periods (in this case, days) in the future is the average of the highest high (375.85) and the lowest low (292.5) of the past 52 periods**

Now, this is what Senkou B tells us:

- If Senkou B is rising in the future, the stock is considered bullish.

- If, on the other hand, Senkou B is declining in the future, then the chart is considered bearish.

Like Senkou A, the current Senkou B can also provide support and resistance to the stock price (*see* Figure 2.17 and Figure 2.18). This support or resistance is especially strong if Senkou B is trending horizontal. Keep in mind that it is a longer term equilibrium point.

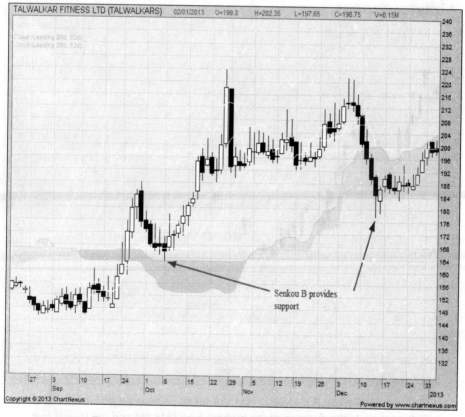

Figure 2.17: **Senkou B providing support to the price**

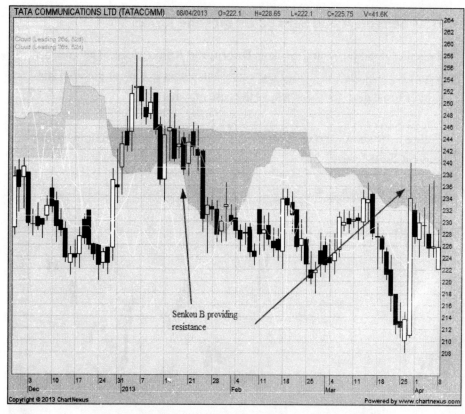

Figure 2.18: **Senkou B offering resistance to the price**

What Senkou A and Senkou B Tell Us About the Trend

- **If Senkou A is above Senkou B, it is considered bullish.**

- **If Senkou A is below Senkou B, it is considered bearish.**

The reason for this is simple. The Senkou A is a faster averaging indicator compared to Senkou B. Thus, when a stock is rising, Senkou A will have higher values than would Senkou B. Conversely, when prices are declining, Senkou A by definition will move faster and decline before Senkou B does.

How Senkou A and Senkou B Form the Kumo

Together, Senkou A and Senkou B form the Kumo cloud. The area between the two lines is shaded and represents either a zone of possible support or resistance, for the stock, as the case may be.

Figure 2.19 shows the chart of Sun TV. Notice how the Kumo provides support for the price.

Figure 2.19: **Kumo is the shaded are in the chart, formed by Senkou A and Senkou B**

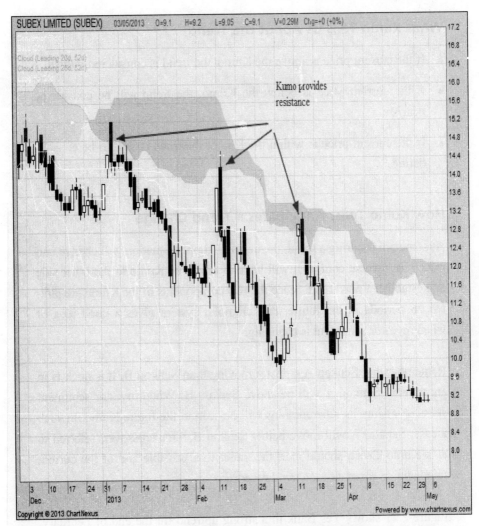

Figure 2.20: **The resistance offered by the downtrending Kumo keeps the price rally in check**

Figure 2.20 depicts the chart of Subex. In this case, the downtrending Kumo offers resistance to every price rally.

What Kumo Tells Us About the Trend

- If the current price is above the Kumo, the trend is considered bullish.

- If the current price is below the Kumo, the trend will be considered bearish.

- If the current price is within the Kumo, the trend is said to be consolidating.

How Kumo Twist Anticipates a Trend Change

At some point during a trend, the demand-supply equation will change and price will reverse course. It will have to cross the Kumo to the other side and establish a new trend. Since the two components of the Kumo are plotted 26 periods in the future, the Ichimoku system gives a good idea of when investor sentiment is changing.

Remember that Senkou A is faster moving than Senkou B. If a stock is in an uptrend, Senkou A will be above Senkou B. When investor sentiment starts reversing, its repercussions will be seen in the future Kumo. In such a case, Senkou A will move below Senkou B. This crossover, referred to as a Kumo Twist, should alert the trader to a possible end of the current trend and, in some cases, a trend reversal.

Figure 2.21 shows Yes Bank in a strong uptrend till the end of February. Notice how the Kumo was rising during this period with Senkou A above Senkou B. However, at the end of February, the future Kumo had a bearish twist. This would have alerted traders that the current uptrend might be over and that it might be time to liquidate the entire position.

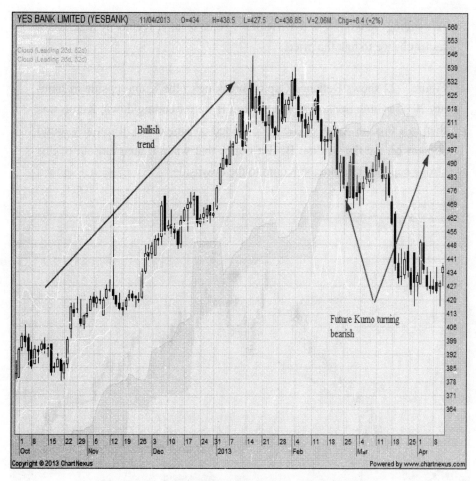

Figure 2.21: **Future Kumo forewarns of trend change**

Traders should also keep in mind that price will have relative ease in breaking through to the other side of the Kumo if the Kumo's width is thin.

A flat Senkou B can provide strong support / resistance to the price depending on the nature of approach.

A flat Senkou B means a steady equilibrium of prices.

A trending Senkou A and B, which I refer to as a Kumo in flux, has a lesser chance to halt the price.

Figure 2.22 shows Reliance Capital breaking to the Kumo upside in January 2012 as both Senkou A and Senkou B were trending down; Kumo was then in a flux. In April, as the price started coming down, it initially found support on the flat Senkou B. But notice that when it then ran out of this strong support, it broke the Kumo to the downside.

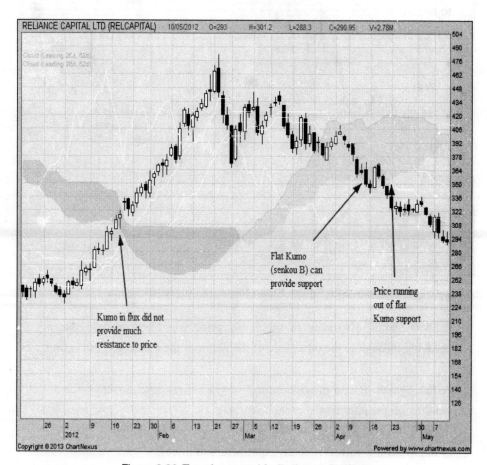

Figure 2.22: **Trend reversal in Reliance Capital**

Chikou

The Chikou is a simple yet powerful component of Ichimoku. It is the curret price shifted back 26 periods.

The Chikou is also the most misunderstood indicator of the Ichimoku system. Its simple nature masks its immense potential. Many traders disregard it on their charts either for a lack of understanding or because they think it to be too simple to be useful. Do not make this mistake. **Chikou provides powerful information to the trader** as you will witness. Here is how:

- **If Chikou is above the price of 26 days ago, then the chart is bullish.**

- **If Chikou is below the price of 26 days ago, it is considered bearish.**

Figure 2.23 shows a bearish chart.

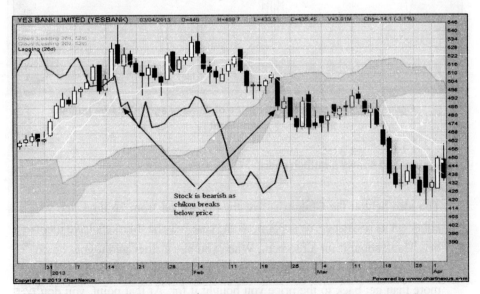

Figure 2.23: **Chikou below the price of 26 days ago indicates bearish sentiment**

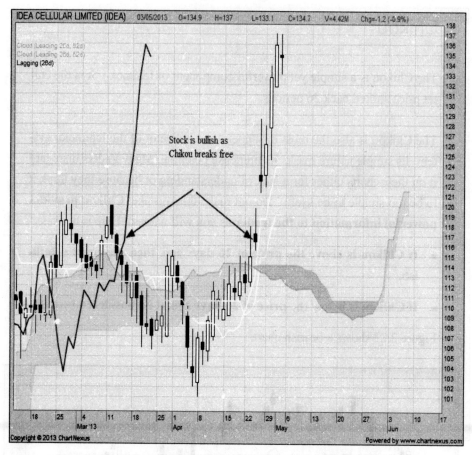

Figure 2.24: **Chikou above the price of 26 days ago indicates bullish sentiment**

Figure 2.24 shows a bullish chart.

The idea behind the Chikou is that the price level from 26 days ago will either act as resistance, or support, as the case may be. Markets have memory. Think about it for a moment. When you buy a stock and it goes down, what do you hope for? A breakeven! You want the stock to do nothing more than get back to the price you bought it for. At that point, you don't

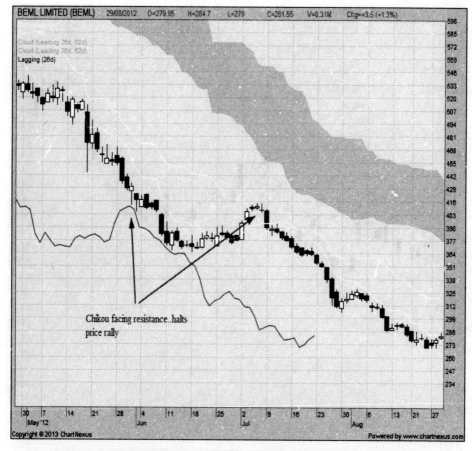

Figure 2.25: **Chikou facing resistance from 26 days prior candles**

care about making even a single rupee. All you want is your hard earned money, your capital, back. This creates a supply zone / resistance zone for the stock. For example, for the stock to go any higher in Figure 2.25, demand will have to overcome the available supply.

A corresponding scenario holds true for the reverse side. If you either shorted a stock or missed buying it at a particular level, and the stock has now come back to the same level, wouldn't you want either to cover the

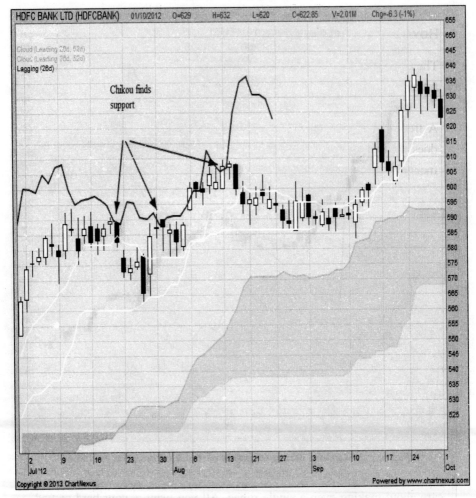

Figure 2.26: **Chikou finds support on candles from 26 days ago**

short or jump into the stock at this point, as the case may be. Most likely you will. This creates a demand zone, or support zone, for the stock (*see* Figure 2.26). For the stock to go lower, this demand will have to be over-whelmed by the supply.

How Chikou Acts as a Momentum Indicator

The Chikou is a good indication of how the trend will proceed in the near future.

A trend has a good chance of running as long as the Chikou is free and does not run into previous prices. In this sense, the Chikou acts as a momentum indicator as illustrated in Figure 2.27.

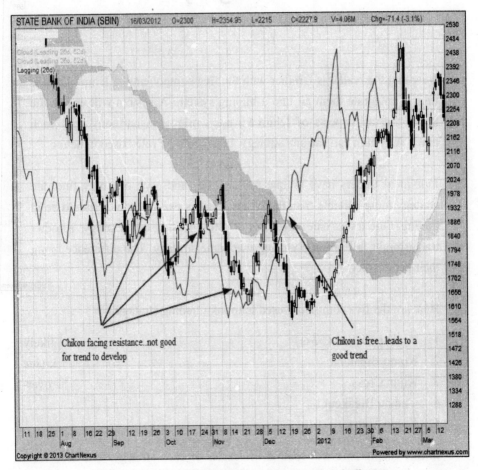

Figure 2.27: **How Chikou acts as a momentum indicator**

3

Ichimoku Trading System

Now that the reader is familiar with the five components of Ichimoku, it is time to integrate them all into a trading system. A system will ensure the trader that all aspects of Ichimoku are working in harmony with each other. A system can use any strategy, but should be rule-based in nature.

Individual traders have unique personalities and each one may find one strategy more suitable than the others. That is exactly how it should be in trading. One trader can make tens of million using one strategy. Another trader might fail miserably using that same strategy. The difference being their personality.

Here are the five commonly used Ichimoku trading strategies.

1. Tenkan / Kijun Cross.
2. Kumo Breakout.
3. Kijun Cross.
4. Chikou Breakout.
5. Kumo Twist.

In this chapter, we will look at the basics of each strategy. The first two strategies are then further discussed in depth, and with many, many examples in Chapters 4 and 5. They are my favorite strategies and work with an extremely high degree of success. If you wish to use the other three strategies, you can design rules similar to the ones described for the first two.

Alert

Keep in mind that no matter what underlying strategy one uses for entry into a position, all the Ichimoku components need to be looked at for their bearish or bullish indications. This can't be emphasized enough.

Tenkan / Kijun Cross Strategy (T/K Cross)

Basic Principle

- Long positions are initiated when the Tenkan crosses the Kijun to the upside.

- Short positions are initiated when the Tenkan crosses the Kijun to the downside.

According to Ichimoku, the effectiveness of the T/K cross depends on its location with respect to the Kumo:

- If a bullish T/K cross occurs above the Kumo, it is considered a strong bullish signal.

- If a bullish T/K cross occurs below the Kumo, it is considered a weak bullish signal.

- If a bullish T/K cross occurs within the Kumo, it is considered a neutral bullish signal.

Correspondingly, on the bearish side:

- If a bearish T/K cross occurs above the Kumo, it is considered a weak bearish signal.

- If a bearish T/K cross occurs below the Kumo, it is considered a strong bearish signal.

- If a bearish T/K cross occurs within the Kumo, it is considered a neutral bearish signal.

Let us look at each example that follows to understand these points clearly.

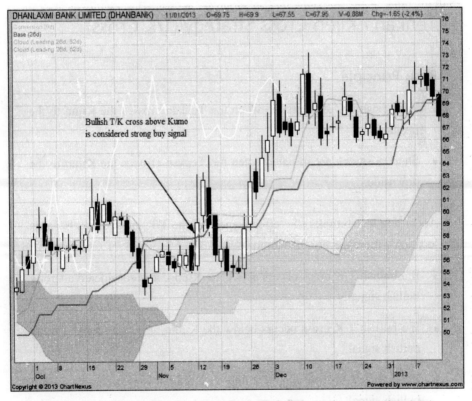

Figure 3.1: **Strong bullish signal as the bullish T/K cross occurs above the Kumo cloud**

Figure 3.1 shows a strong bullish T/K cross because it occurred above the Kumo.

Figure 3.2 shows a weak bullish T/K cross because it occurred below the Kumo.

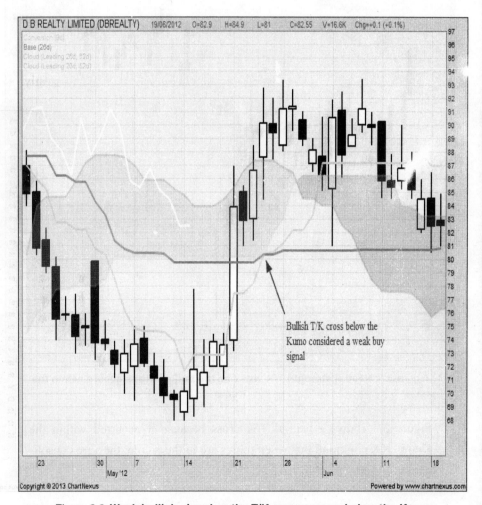

Figure 3.2: **Weak bullish signal as the T/K cross occurs below the Kumo**

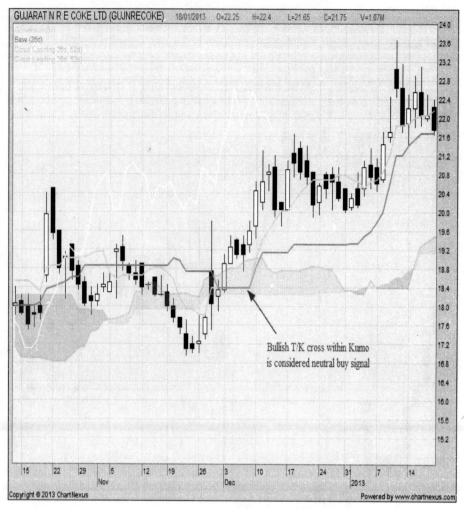

Figure 3.3: **Neutral strength T/K cross as the bullish cross occurs within the Kumo**

Figure 3.3 shows a neutral T/K cross because it occurred within the Kumo. Keep in mind that when things are in the Kumo, they are consolidating.

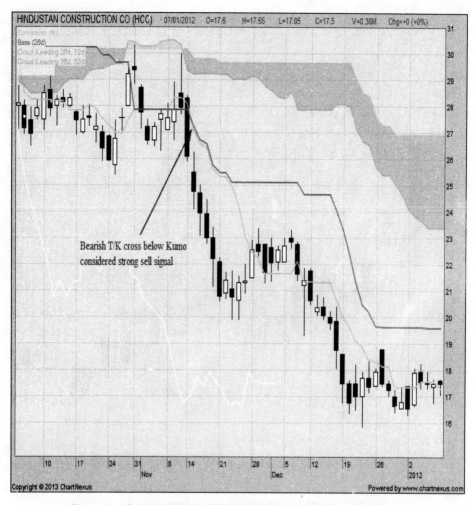

Figure 3.4: **Strong bearish T/K cross occurring below the Kumo**

Figure 3.4 shows a strongly bearish T/K cross because it occurred below the Kumo.

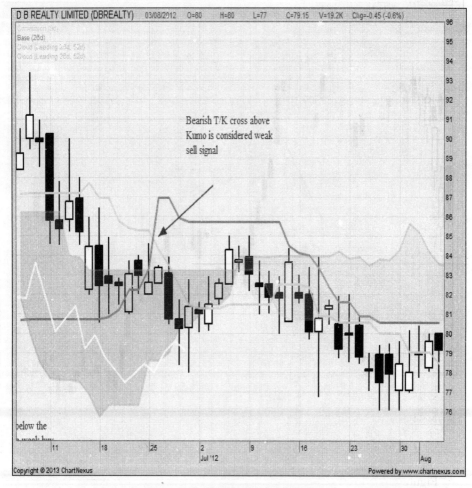

Figure 3.5: **Weak bearish T/K cross**

Figure 3.5 shows a weak bearish T/K cross because it occurred above the Kumo.

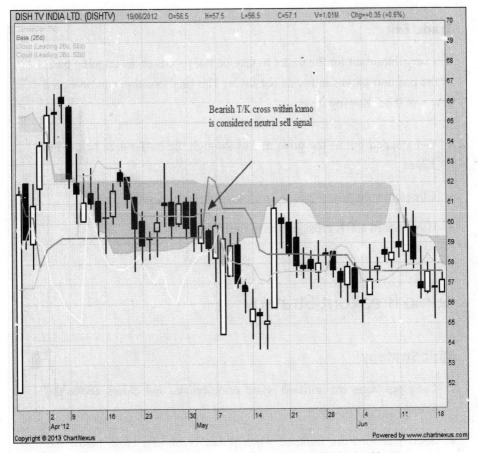

Figure 3.6: **Neutral T/K cross as the cross is within the Kumo**

Figure 3.6 shows a neutral bearish T/K cross as it occurred within the Kumo.

Stop Setting

Initially the stop loss is set, with a small buffer, above or below the Kijun depending upon if the trade is bearish or bullish, respectively. As the position moves in the anticipated direction, it will continue to draw the Kijun with it. This enables the trader to trail one's stop out level with the Kijun.

Trade Exit

It is very important for the trader to take partial profits on an ongoing basis as the position moves in his or her favor. The final position can be exited in any of the following ways:

- Get stopped out as the price moves through the buffer area below the Kijun.

- Close out your position as price closes below the Kijun.

- Close out of a T/K cross occurs in the opposite direction.

Kumo Breakout Strategy

Basic Strategy

- Long positions are initiated when price breaks and closes above the Kumo.

- Short positions are initiated when prices break and close below the Kumo.

As mentioned earlier, the Kumo is central to Ichimoku. When prices are above the Kumo, the chart is considered bullish and when prices are below the Kumo, the chart is considered bearish. The chart in Figure 3.7 shows a long position entry as the price closes above the Kumo.

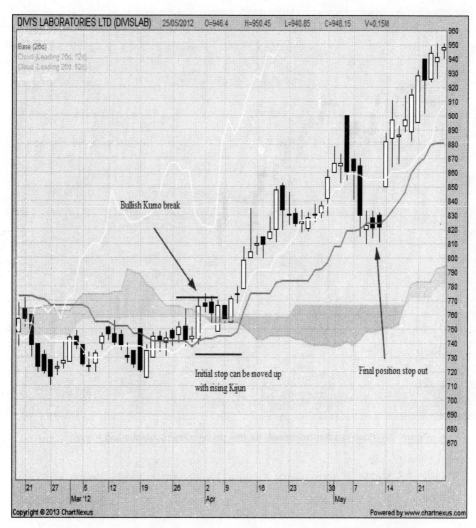

Figure 3.7: **Bullish Kumo break as the price closes above the Kumo**

Figure 3.7 shows a bullish Kumo break. Traders can enter a long position on strength, meaning above the high of the signal candle.

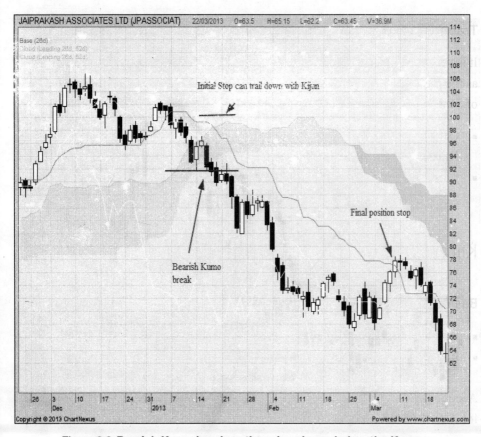

Figure 3.8: **Bearish Kumo break as the price closes below the Kumo**

Figure 3.8 shows a short entry scenario as the price closes below the Kumo.

Stop Setting

Initially the stop loss is set either above or below the Kijun with a small buffer depending upon if the trade is bearish or bullish, respectively. As the position moves in the anticipated direction, it will continue to draw the Kijun with it. This enables the trader to trail his or her stop out level with the Kijun.

Trade Exit

It is very important for the trader to take partial profits on an ongoing basis as the position moves in his favor. The final position can be exited in any of the following ways:

- Get stopped out as the price moves through the buffer area beyond the Kijun.
- Close out the position as price closes above / below the Kijun.

Kijun Cross

Basic Strategy

- Initiate long position when price closes above the Kijun.
- Initiate short position when price closes below the Kijun.

According to Ichimoku, the effectiveness of the Kijun cross depends on its location with respect to the Kumo.

- If price closes above the Kijun and this crossover is above the Kumo, it is considered a strong bullish signal.

- If price closes above the Kijun but the crossover is below the Kumo, it is considered a weak bullish signal.

- If the price closes above Kijun and it is within the Kumo, it is considered a neutral bullish signal.

Correspondingly, on the bearish side:

- If the price closes below the Kijun and it is below the Kumo, it is considered a strong bearish signal.

- If the price closes below Kijun and it is above the Kumo, it is considered a weak bearish signal.

- If the price closes below Kijun and it is within the Kumo, it is considered a neutral bearish signal.

Let's review the charts below for understanding these nuances.

Figure 3.9 shows Price / Kijun cross in the chart of Jaiprakash Power. Since the cross is above the Kumo, a strong bullish signal.

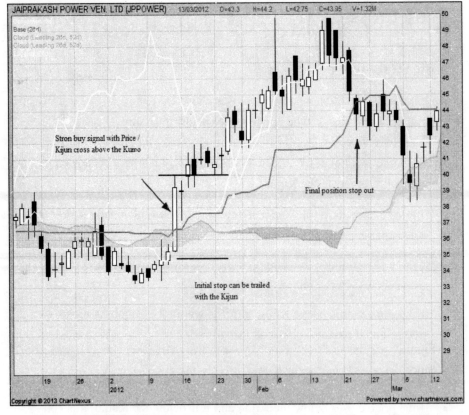

Figure 3.9: **Strong bullish signal as the price crossover of Kijun is above the Kumo**

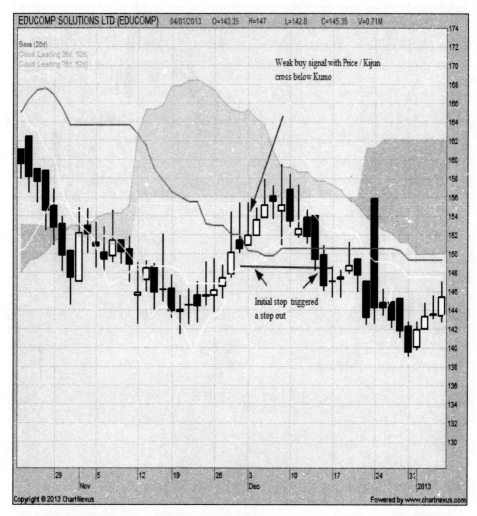

Figure 3.10: **Weak bullish signal as the price crossover of Kijun is below the Kumo**

Figure 3.10 shows Price / Kijun cross in the chart of Educomp Solutions. Since the cross is below the Kumo, it is a weak bullish signal.

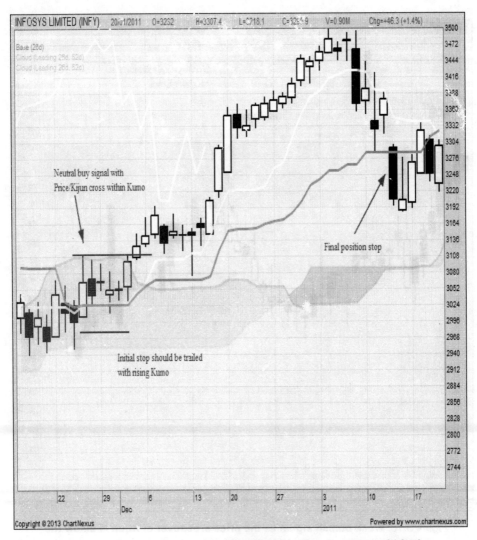

Figure 3.11: **Neutral bullish price Kijun crossover as it occurs within the Kumo**

Figure 3.11 shows a neutral bullish price / Kijun cross in the chart of Infosys, as the cross occurs within the Kumo.

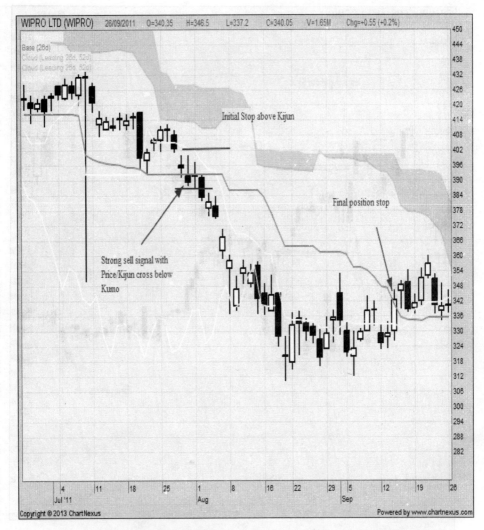

Figure 3.12: **Strong bearish price cross with Kijun below the Kumo**

Figure 3.12 shows a strong bearish price / Kijun cross in the chart of Wipro, with Kijun below the Kumo.

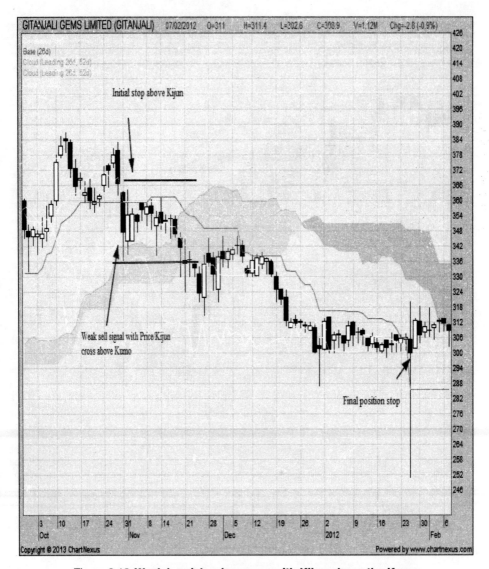

Figure 3.13: **Weak bearish price cross with Kijun above the Kumo**

Figure 3.13 shows a weak bearish price / Kijun cross, with the Kijun being above the Kumo in the chart of Gitanjali Gems.

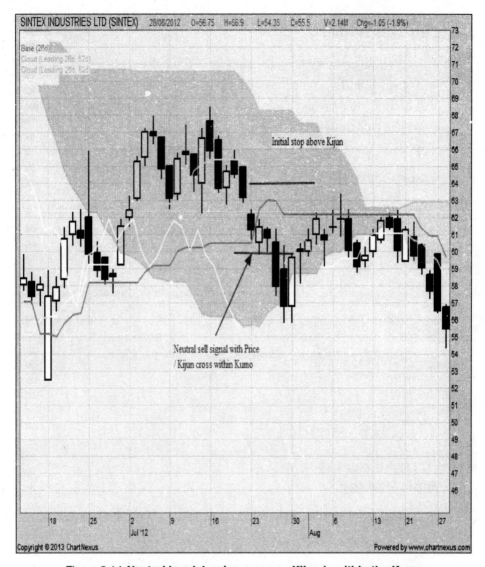

Figure 3.14: **Neutral bearish price cross as Kijun is within the Kumo**

Figure 3.14 shows a neutral bearish price / Kijun cross in Sintex, as the Kijun is within the Kumo.

Stop Loss Setting

For the Kijun cross strategy, the stop loss is initially set below the Kijun with a small buffer. As the position moves in the anticipated direction, it will continue to draw the Kijun with it. This enables the trader to trail his stop level with the Kijun.

Trade Exit

It is very important for the trader to take partial profits on an ongoing basis as the position moves in his favor. The final position can be exited in any of the following ways:

- Get stopped out as the price moves through the buffer area below the Kijun.

- Close out position when the price closes below the Kijun.

Chikou Breakout

Basic Strategy

- Initiate long position when Chikou crosses and closes above the price of 26 days ago.

- Initiate short position when Chikou crosses and closes below the price of 26 days ago.

As a trader you should visually ascertain if there will be any immediate resistance to the Chikou within the next few trading periods as the current price moves up or down. This is important because the Chikou needs to be free for the trend to continue.

According to Ichimoku, the effectiveness of the Chikou cross, or breakout, depends on the location of the current price with respect to the Kumo.

- If the Chikou closes above the price of 26 days ago, and the current price is above the Kumo, it is considered a strong bullish signal.

- If the Chikou closes above the price of 26 days ago, but the current price is below the Kumo, it is considered a weak bullish signal.

- If the Chikou closes above the price of 26 days ago, and the current price is within the Kumo, it is considered a neutral bullish signal.

Correspondingly, on the bearish side:

- If the Chikou closes below the price of 26 days ago, and the current price is below the Kumo, it is considered a strong bearish signal.

- If the Chikou closes below the price of 26 days ago, but the current price is above the Kumo, it is considered a weak bearish signal.

- If the Chikou closes below the price of 26 days ago and the current price is within the Kumo, it is considered a neutral bearish signal.

The examples that follow depict the different scenarios listed above.

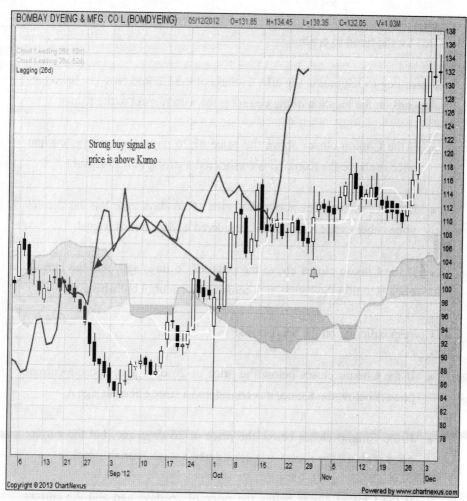

Figure 3.15: **Strong bullish signal — the Chikou crosses above the price of 26 days ago, and the current price is above the Kumo**

Figure 3.15 shows the chart of Bombay Dyeing displaying a strong buy signal as the Chikou crosses above the price of 26 days ago, and the current price is above the Kumo.

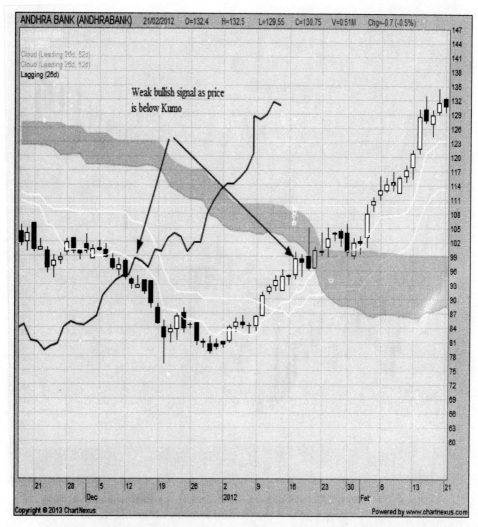

Figure 3.16: **Weak bullish signal as the Chikou crosses above the price from 26 days ago but the current price is below the Kumo**

The Andhra Bank chart in Figure 3.16 shows a weak buy signal as the Chikou crosses above the price from 26 days ago but the current price is below the Kumo.

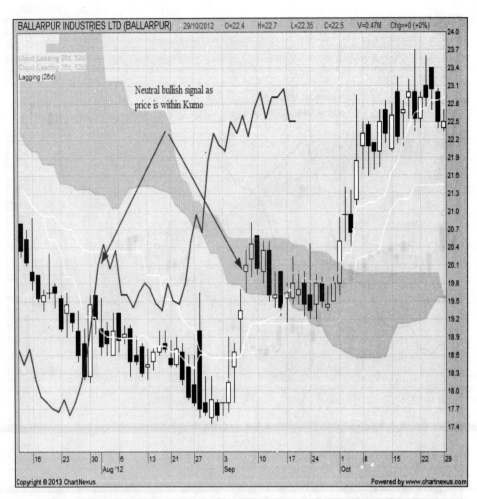

Neutral bullish signal as price is within Kumo

Figure 3.17: **Neutral bullish signal — the Chikou crosses above the price from 26 days ago and the current price is within the Kumo**

The Ballarpur Industries chart in Figure 3.17 shows a neutral buy signal as the Chikou crosses above the price from 26 days ago while the current price is within the Kumo.

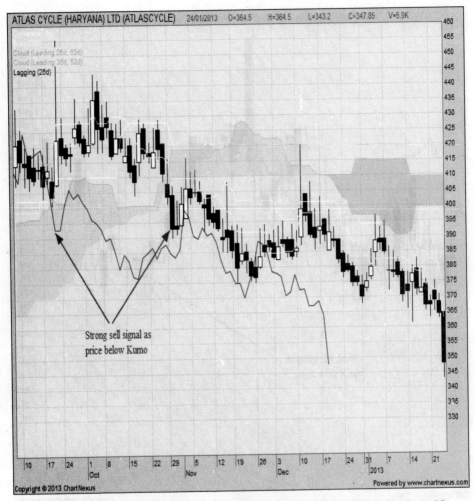

Figure 3.18: **Strong sell signal — the Chikou crosses below the price from 26 days ago and the current price is below the Kumo**

The Atlas Cycle chart in Figure 3.18 shows a strong sell signal as the Chikou crosses below the price from 26 days ago and the current price is below the Kumo.

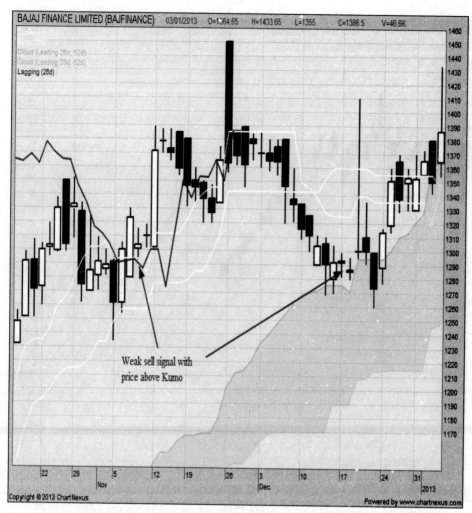

Figure 3.19: **Weak sell signal — the Chikou crosses below the price from 26 days ago and the current price is above the Kumo**

The Bajaj Finance chart in Figure 3.19 shows a weak sell signal as the Chikou crosses below the price from 26 days ago but the current price is above the Kumo.

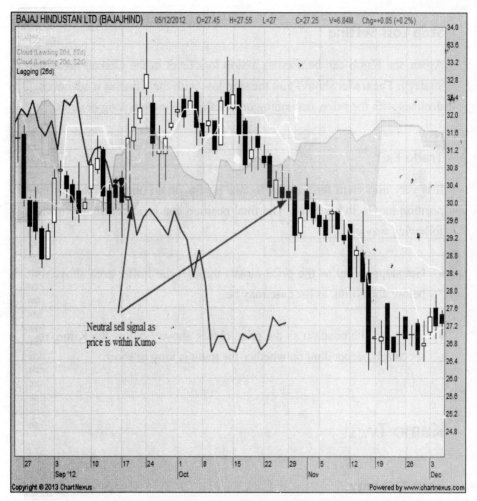

Figure 3.20: **Neutral sell signal — the Chikou crosses below the price from 26 days ago and the current price is within the Kumo**

The Bajaj Hindustan chart in Figure 3.20 shows a neutral sell signal as the Chikou crosses below the price from 26 days ago while the current price is within the Kumo.

Stop Loss Setting

Again, the Kijun can be used as a stop loss level in the Chikou breakout strategy. The trader should trail the stop loss with the Kijun as it advances / declines with the price, depending on whether the trade is long or short.

Trade Exit

It is very important for a trader to take profits on an ongoing basis as the position moves in his favor. The final position can be exited in any of the following ways:

- Get stopped out as the price moves through the buffer area above, or below, the Kijun, as the case may be.

- Close out the position as the price closes above / below the Kijun, respectively, depending on whether the trade is long or short.

Kumo Twist

Basic Strategy

- A long position is initiated when the future Kumo turns from bearish to bullish.

- Conversely, a short position is initiated when the future Kumo turns from bullish to bearish.

This basically implies that to enter a long position Senkou A should cross Senkou B to the upside in the future. On the other hand, in order to enter a short position, Senkou A should cross Senkou B to the downside in the future.

According to Ichimoku, the effectiveness of the Kumo twist depends location of the current price with respect to the Kumo.

Thus, on the bullish side:

- If the bullish future Kumo twist occurs when the current price is above the Kumo, it is considered a strong bullish signal.

- If the bullish future Kumo twist occurs when the current price is below the Kumo, it is considered a weak bullish signal.

- If the bullish future Kumo twist occurs when the current price is within the Kumo, it is considered a neutral bullish signal.

On the bearish side:

- If the bearish future Kumo twist occurs when the current price is below the Kumo, it is considered a strong bearish signal.

- If the bearish future Kumo twist occurs when the current price is above the Kumo, it is considered a weak bearish signal.

- If the bearish future Kumo twist occurs when the current price is within the Kumo, it is considered a neutral bearish signal.

The charts that follow will illustrate the above scenarios.

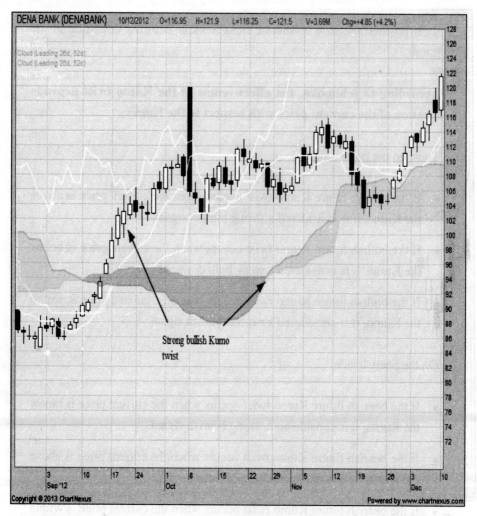

Figure 3.21: **Strong bullish Kumo twist signal — the current price is above the current Kumo**

The Dena Bank chart in Figure 3.21 shows a bullish future Kumo twist. As the current price is above the current Kumo, so this would be considered a strong bullish signal.

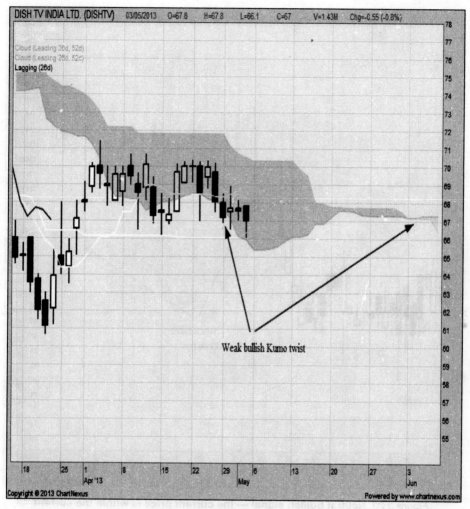

Figure 3.22: **Weak bullish Kumo twist signal — the current price is below the current Kumo**

Figure 3.22 shows a bullish future Kumo twist in the chart of Dish TV. The current price is below the current Kumo, so this would be considered a weak bullish signal.

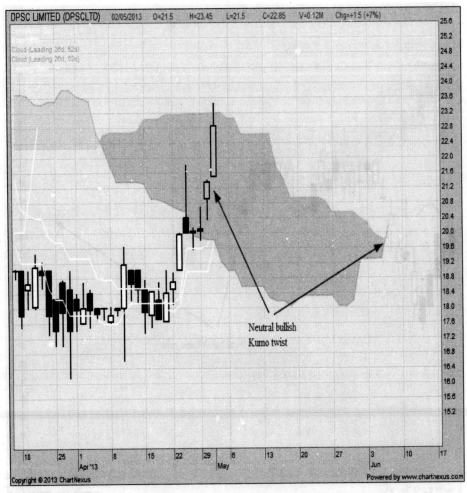

Figure 3.23: **Neutral bullish signal — the current price is within the current Kumo**

Figure 3.23 shows a bullish future Kumo twist in the chart of DPSC Ltd. The current price is within the current Kumo, so this would be considered a neutral bullish signal.

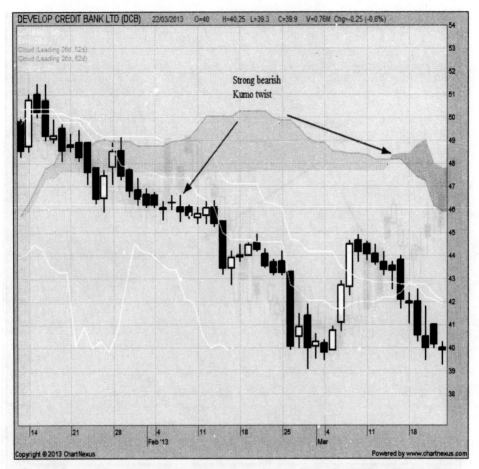

Figure 3.24: **Strong bearish signal — the current price is below the current Kumo**

Figure 3.24 shows a bearish future Kumo twist in the chart of Development Credit Bank Ltd. The current price is below the current Kumo, so this would be considered a strong bearish signal.

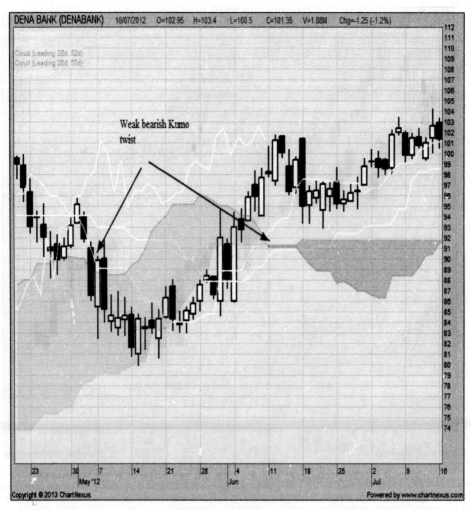

Figure 3.25: **Weak bearish signal — the current price is above the current Kumo**

Figure 3.25 shows a bearish future Kumo twist in the chart of Dena Bank. The current price is above the current Kumo, so this would be considered a weak bearish signal.

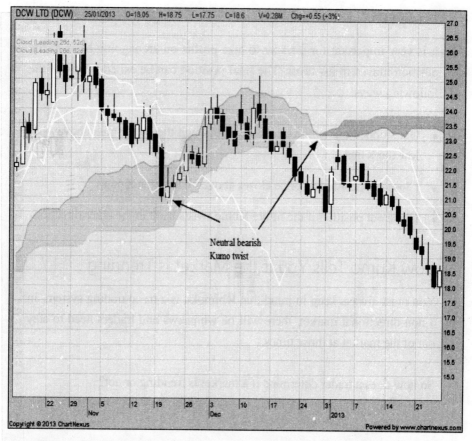

Figure 3.26: **Neutral bearish signal — the current price is within the current Kumo**

Figure 3.26 shows a bearish future Kumo twist in the chart of DCW Ltd. The current price is within the current Kumo, so this would be considered a neutral bearish signal.

Stop Loss Setting

The Kijun can be used as a stop loss with a small buffer. As prices move in the anticipated direction, the Kijun starts trending and the stop can be moved along with it.

Trade Exit

It is very important for a trader to take profits on an ongoing basis as the position moves in his favor. The final position can be exited in any of the following ways:

- Get stopped out as the price moves through the buffer area above / below the Kijun

- Close out position as price closes above / below the Kijun

- Close out position if the future Kumo twists back in the other direction.

How Kumo Tells You if the Market is Trending

You must always keep in mind that Ichimoku is a trend trading system. In a non-directional market, there will be whipsaws and traders need to stay out of the market at those times.

So how does a trader determine if a market is trending or not?

Look at the Kumo.

- In a bullish trending market, the Kumo will be rising steadily (*see* Figure 3.27).

- In a bearish trending market, the Kumo will be falling steadily.

- In a non-trending market, the Kumo will switch between bearish and bullish in a short period of time as seen in Figure 3.28.

Figure 3.27: **A rising Kumo indicates a bullish trending market**

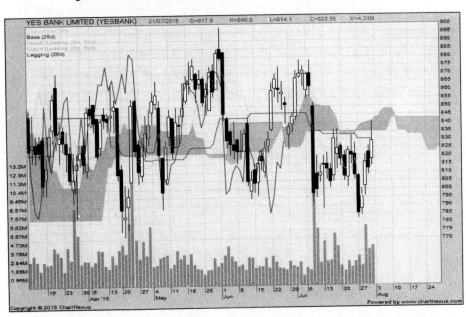

Figure 3.28: **Non-trending market — see how the Kumo goes from bearish to bullish — and *vice versa***

All Ichimoku Components Need to Be Reviewed

It is important to emphasize here that no matter which Ichimoku trading strategy one follows, all the Ichimoku components need to be reviewed. **Trades should not be initiated if individual components of the Ichimoku are in conflict with one another.** There are always good opportunities to trade if you are patient. These strategies can be used on different asset classes and present a wide range of trading possibilities. There is no need to rush into positions by overlooking conflicts between the Ichimoku components. Even though some of the above scenarios depict a neutral or weak signal, I have seen wonderful results initiating trades in those areas. The key is to put together all the components and analyze the overall picture.

In the chapters that follow, particularly Chapter 4 and Chapter 5, we will look at numerous real-life examples of the different Ichimoku trading strategies in action. The readers may notice some repetition as we evaluate the charts. This is deliberate. Such repetition will train your eyes to visually recognize the different trading set-ups and your mind to consistently analyze the complete picture. This is imperative for your trading success.

4

Kumo Break Strategy

As highlighted in the previous chapter, the Kumo break strategy is a very powerful way of using the Ichimoku system.

Basic Strategy

To recapitulate the strategy:

- Long positions are initiated when price breaks, and closes, above the Kumo.

- Short positions are initiated when price breaks, and closes, below the Kumo.

Though one can take this raw strategy and implement it with a certain degree of success, the high probability success factor would be lacking. To turn the Kumo break strategy into a high probability trade, we need to add some rules to it. Rules define the exact conditions for entry into the stock, currency, bond commodity, or any other tradable liquid instrument.

Rules / Conditions

Price *versus* Current Kumo

For this strategy, the price would obviously have to close above the current Kumo. However, the trader also needs to evaluate the nature of the Kumo itself. Is it flat? This question will decide the probability of price continuing its trajectory. Flat Kumos, and most of the time it will be Senkou B, attract prices back to themselves. Remember that Senkou B is the 52-week equilibrium. If prices are trying to break out of this equilibrium, especially without strong support from the Tenkan and Kijun, chances are that they will be drawn back to the Kumo. In a flat Kumo breakout case, therefore, you need to observe how many days in the future does the flatness of the Kumo disappear. If it does so in the next few days, then the trade has a good chance of success. If Senkou B is expected to be flat for quite some time and the Tenkan / Kijun support is far behind the price, the probability of success is reduced.

Direction of the Future Kumo

Is the future Kumo sentiment the same as the direction one is trading in?

- If the trader is planning a bullish trade as the price closes above the Kumo, then the future Kumo should be bullish.

- If the trader is planning to take on a bearish trade as price closes below the Kumo, then the future Kumo should be bearish.

It would be ideal for Senkou A and Senkou B to be both heading in the same direction as the trade. But as long as they are displaying the same sentiment, the indicator would be confirming the trade. There are times when the trader can be a little proactive and enter a trade even if the future Kumo is of the opposite sentiment. This can be contemplated only if all other Ichimoku components are aligned and it can be visually ascertained that a

Kumo twist is likely in the next couple of days. This anticipation of Kumo twist is easy to do as a trader gets more and more accustomed to reading Ichimoku charts.

For example, consider you are making a bullish trade using this strategy. All Ichimoku components are aligned, except that the future Kumo is bearish. At this point, you might visually notice that Senkou A is heading to intersect Senkou B, but the twist has not occurred yet. To anticipate the next couple of days, look to see how the Tenkan and Kijun will be moving in this timeframe. Is the prior 9-period low going to rise higher? Is the prior 26-period low going to rise higher? Any of these conditions will make either the Tenkan or Kijun to go up. That would, in turn, make Senkou A go up some more. Next, check if the prior 52-period highs are expected to drop. If they are, then Senkou B will drop further. Both these conditions will accelerate the Kumo twist and lead to a bullish future Kumo.

Chikou

Do not make the mistake of ignoring this simple indicator. It is the key to your success. When the price closes above the Kumo, visually check the position of Chikou in reference to the price 26 days ago. Is the Chikou below that price? If yes, then the trade cannot be initiated at this time. Even if Chikou is above the price of 26 days ago, but it is visually noticed that it would bump into that price in the next few days if the current price consolidates then, too, the trade should not be entered into.

Essentially, the Chikou should be free and clear of immediate price congestion.

Keep in mind that the Chikou needs to have a closing price above the candle of 26 day ago to give the trade the green light. There would be times when the current price rallies intraday, only to fall back towards the end of the day as Chikou faces resistance from the price 26 days earlier. Wait for the confirmed freedom of Chikou.

Tenkan and Kijun

What is the position of Tenkan *versus* Kijun? If Tenkan is above the Kijun, then the trade has a green light for a bullish entry. Tenkan will need to be below the Kijun for entering a short position. There might be cases where the Tenkan and Kijun are not in the right order, but the trader can visually assess that the Tenkan will cross the Kijun the next day. For a bullish entry case, this might be where the prior 9-period lows are getting higher, while the prior 26-period high / lows are constant. As you get a firm grasp of such visual analysis, your entry points would become more aggressive and profitable. For beginners, it is recommended to wait for the actual confirmation of indicators.

Price *versus* the Tenkan and Kijun

For a bullish trade the price needs to be above the Tenkan and Kijun. For a bearish trade the price needs to be below the Tenkan and Kijun.

That is a simple requirement. However, it would be worthwhile to reiterate here again that the price does not like to be too far away from the Kijun, especially a flat Kijun. If the price has exploded recently and closed above the Kumo leaving the Kijun far behind, there is a high chance that it will retrace and find its equilibrium at the Kijun. Of course there will be trades that keep going higher and drag the Kijun along with them, but those are exceptions. So keep a watch on the conditions that will cause the Kijun to move up.

Trade Entry

Once all the components of the Ichimoku indicator are aligned, the trader places a buy order to buy on strength. This means buying above the high of the control candle, the candle which has the highest high of the previous 9 days. This will ensure that the Tenkan will be pulled in the direction of the trade.

I like to use the Kijun as the initial stop. Some traders use the Average True Range (ATR) indicator to decide the buffer below the Kijun at which the stop is placed. The ATR provides a dynamic stop loss below the Kijun based on the volatility of the stock. As the stock moves in the desired direction, the Kijun will start moving too. This allows the stop to be raised, or lowered, as the case may be, to first reduce the loss and then to lock in profits.

Kumo Break Trading Strategy in Action

The charts that follow, namely from Figure 4.1 to Figure 4.23, show the Kumo break trading strategy in action. I have described the real-life scenarios in some detail in the initial few charts and, then for the rest, I have highlighted the key indicators that need to be looked at.

I have also included charts where the trade would have resulted in a loss. This is to be expected. Losing is part of the trading game. There is no system which will give 100% win results. The idea is to keep losses small and let profits run.

Example 4.1: Going Long Using the Kumo Break Strategy

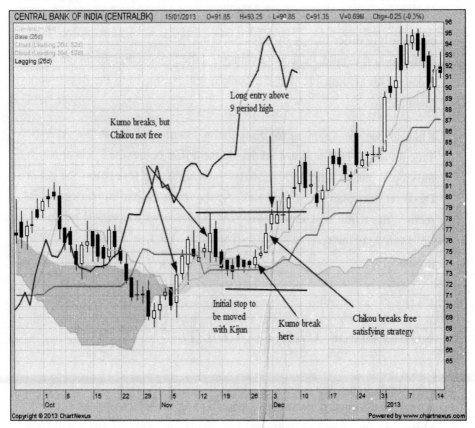

Figure 4.1: **Going long as three Kumo bullish breaks show up in the chart of Central Bank of India**

Trade Set-up

The chart of Central Bank of India in Figure 4.1 shows three bullish Kumo breaks in 2012. The first two, on 6 November and 15 November, respectively, did not satisfy our criteria for a long entry. One can see that the Chikou was still under the price congestion from 26 days ago for these two Kumo breaks. As we've learnt, Chikou is indicative of the trend's strength.

As current prices bump against the price level of 26 days ago, sellers flood the market with supply causing a pullback in prices.

Entry

The third bullish Kumo break occurred on 27 November. Chikou was still not clear of price congestion and the stock at this point was below the Tenkan. This meant another wait in store for the trader looking for the right set up conditions! A couple of days later, however, the price climbed and closed above the Tenkan. This also caused Chikou to break out of the price from 26 days ago. With the future Kumo cloud bullish and Tenkan above the Kijun, all of our Ichimoku conditions were satisfied for a long entry above the 9-period high.

Notice in the chart that the 26-period high is not too far compared to the 9-period high. Wouldn't you want the Kijun to also move up in support of the stock along with the Tenkan? As an Ichimoku system follower, that would be the correct strategy. So the buy order would be placed above the 26-period high and would have been triggered on 3 December.

Stop Loss

The initial stop loss would be placed below the Kijun with a buffer. As the price starts to move higher in the anticipated direction, it will draw the Kijun upwards with it. This allows the trader to keep moving the stop up.

Exit

Partial profits should be taken along the way as the price rises and the final position should be stopped out when the stock closes below the Kijun, or trades through the buffer below the Kijun.

Example 4.2: Going Long Using the Kumo Break Strategy

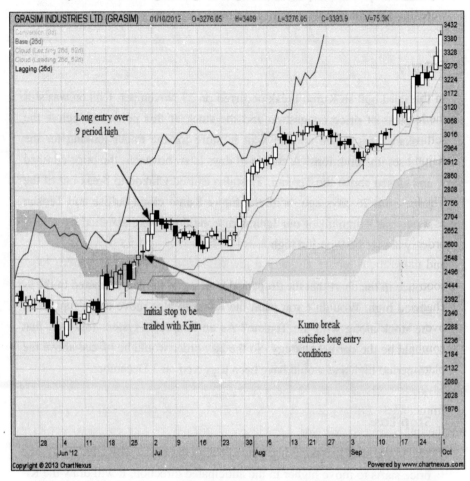

GRASIM INDUSTRIES LTD (GRASIM)   01/10/2012   O=3276.05   H=3409   L=3276.05   C=3393.9   V=75.3K

Long entry over
9 period high

Initial stop to be
trailed with Kijun

Kumo break
satisfies long entry
conditions

Copyright © 2013 ChartNexus   Powered by www.chartnexus.com

Figure 4.2: **Trading long in Grasim Industries — the Kumo break, entry and stop loss points are indicated**

Trade Set-up

The chart in Figure 4.2 shows Grasim Industries closing above the Kumo on 28 June 2012. At this point, Chikou was free of the price action of 26 days ago. The price was above Tenkan and Kijun. Tenkan was above the

Kijun and the future Kumo cloud was bullish. All our Ichimoku conditions were thus satisfied for a long entry above the 9-period high.

Entry

In this case, the 9-period high was the high set on the previous day with the long upper shadow candle. This candle also set the 26-period high. So setting a buy order above this candle's high would ensure that Tenkan and Kijun both move up to support the stock.

The buy order would have triggered on 2 July. Keep in mind that as soon as a position is entered, one also needs to immediately place the stop loss order. This is critical. One cannot decide the stop loss level in one's mind and think about implementing it a few days after the trade is entered. As soon as a trade is executed, the whole emotional dynamics of the trader changes. Rationality goes out of the window as the trader's emotions take over. So put the stop loss order as soon as the trade is executed, or as a combination order if the broker allows. In this case, a sell order would be placed below the Kijun on that date.

Immediately following the buy execution, the price retraces all the way to the uptrending Kijun. Note here that near the 5 July area, the stop should have been moved up below the Kijun at this point.

The Kijun supports the price and the bulls come back in to rally the stock.

Exit

As the price moves up, partial profits should be taken along the way. The final position should be closed out when price closes below the Kijun, or trades through the buffer below the Kijun.

Example 4.3: Going Short Using the Kumo Break Strategy

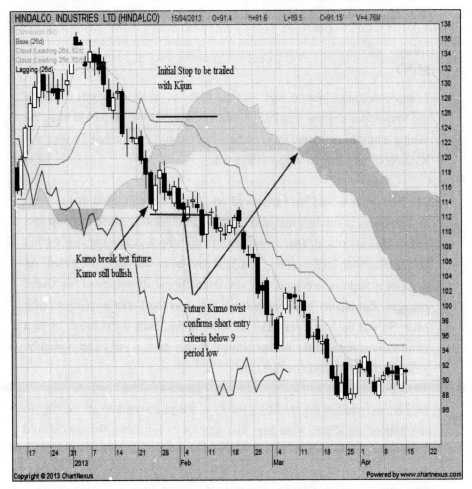

Figure 4.3: **Going short in Hindalco — the Kumo break, the future Kumo and initial stop loss points are indicated**

Trade Set-up for Short Entry on 5 February

Tenkan / Kijun: In the chart in Figure 4.3, Hindalco's price is below the Tenkan and Kijun, which is bearish. Tenkan is below the Kijun, which is also bearish. And, both Tenkan and Kijun will continue to fall as the price goes lower.

Chikou: At the point of entry, Chikou will be clear of any price interaction.

Current Kumo: Prices are below the current Kumo.

Future Kumo: The future Kumo has turned bearish confirming all the other indicators.

Initial Stop: The initial stop will be above the Kijun. This stop can be moved down as the price starts to move lower and Kijun trails downward with it.

Trade Analysis

Hindalco's price closed below the Kumo on 24 January. The Chikou was free at this point, but the future Kumo was still bullish. To enter a short trade, the future Kumo would need to twist. As soon as this happens, a short entry can be placed below the 9-period low. In this case, the 9-period low is the same as the 26-period low. The trader is thus assured that both Tenkan and Kijun will move lower when the trade is executed. Notice also in the chart in Figure 4.3 that the 26-period highs are going to head south soon after the time of entry. This will help the Kijun trend down and the stop loss setting to be moved closer to the price.

Partial profits should continuously be taken as the trade progresses in the expected direction. Final position should be stopped out as the stock closes above the Kijun.

Example 4.4: Going Long Using the Kumo Break Strategy

Figure 4.4: **Going long in Aurobindo Pharma — Kumo break, trade entry and initial stop points are indicated**

Trade Set-up for Long Entry on 3 September

Tenkan / Kijun: The price is above both Tenkan and Kijun, which is a bullish sign. Tenkan is above the Kijun, which is also bullish.

Chikou: At the point of entry, the Chikou will be clear of any price interaction.

Current Kumo: The price is above the current Kumo.

Future Kumo: The future Kumo has turned bullish, thus confirming all the other indicators.

Initial Stop: The initial stop will be below the Kijun. This stop can be moved up as the price starts to move higher and the Kijun also trails upward with it.

Trade Analysis

Aurobindo Pharma's price closed above the thin Kumo on 31 August. At that point, the Chikou was above the price congestion and the future Kumo had turned bullish. All the Ichimoku components were lined up for a long entry above the 9-period high. This would ensure that Tenkan is drawn up to help support the price. Traders can as well place the buy entry at the 26-period high in this case as there is not much difference between the 9-period and 26-period highs. Doing so ensures that even the Kijun is drawn up in the expected direction of the trade. Partial profits should be taken on a regular basis as prices climb, with the final position being stopped out below the Kijun.

Note in the chart that there was a Kumo break on 28 August. This did not, however, satisfy the future Kumo requirement as it was still bearish.

Example 4.5: Going Long Using the Kumo Break Strategy

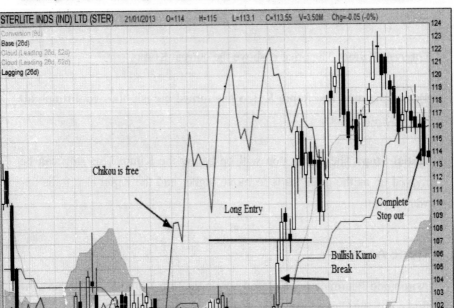

Figure 4.5: **Going long in Sterlite Industries — the bullish Kumo break and long entry points are indicated**

Trade Set-up for Long Entry on 30 November

Tenkan / Kijun: The price is above Tenkan and Kijun, which is bullish. Tenkan is above the Kijun, which is also a bullish sign.

Chikou: At the point of entry, the Chikou will be clear of any price interaction.

Current Kumo: Prices are above the current Kumo.

Future Kumo: The future Kumo is bullish, thus confirming all the other indicators.

Initial Stop: The initial stop should be below the Kijun. This stop can be moved up as the price starts to move higher and the Kijun trails upward with it.

Trade Analysis

This trade needs to be initiated with caution in mind. Even though the chart looks good after the fact, the entry conditions were not very ideal. If you noticed this fact, you are well on your way to being successful at Ichimoku trading. The reason for this cautious outlook is the flat Kumo that the price broke out of. Notice Senkou B is flat for the next 9 days. This equilibrium can very well attract prices back to it. In this particular example, the price rocketed up to draw the Tenkan and Kijun above the Kumo to support it if necessary.

A flat Senkou B is very powerful and should be carefully evaluated. Notice in the chart how the price was rejected twice at this Kumo level in the previous trading month.

Partial profits should be taken on a continuous basis as the price heads in the expected direction. Finally, the position should be completely stopped out as the price closes below the Kijun.

Example 4.6: Going Short Using the Kumo Break Strategy

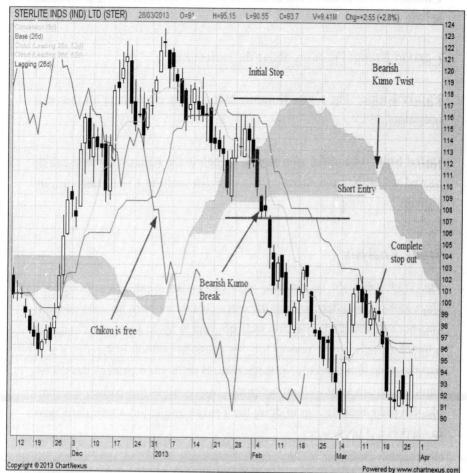

Figure 4.6: **Going short in Sterlite Industries — notice the bearish Kumo break, the free Chikou, the entry point and the initial stop above the Kijun**

Trade Set-up for Short Entry on 7 February

Tenkan / Kijun: The price is below the Tenkan and Kijun, which is a bearish sign. Tenkan is below the Kijun, which is also bearish. And, both Tenkan and Kijun will continue to fall as the price goes lower.

Chikou: At the point of entry, the Chikou will be clear of any price interaction.

Current Kumo: The price is below the current Kumo.

Future Kumo: The future Kumo has turned bearish, thus confirming all the other indicators.

Initial Stop: The initial stop should be above the Kijun. This stop can be moved down as the price starts to move lower and the Kijun trails downward with it.

Trade Analysis

The price of Sterlite closed below the Kumo on 5 February. While the Chikou was free at this point, but the future Kumo was still bullish. The Kumo twist occurred a couple of days later to provide a good short entry signal. In this case placing a sell order below the 9-period low would ensure that the Tenkan and Kijun both move down.

Profits should continuously be taken as the trade progresses in the expected direction. The final position should be stopped out as the stock closes above the Kijun.

Notice in this chart how the flat Senkou B rejected the price on 25 January. The stock bounced right back up to test the Kijun and failed. The price finally ran out of the flat Senkou B when it closed below the Kumo. That one day of Kumo flux was good enough for the price to penetrate to the bearish side. Had the price been one day late, it would have had to contend with another long stretch of flat Senkou B. It is important for the trader to notice these subtleties and analyze them in as much depth as possible to get the confidence to place trades using the Ichimoku system.

Example 4.7: Going Long Using the Kumo Break Strategy

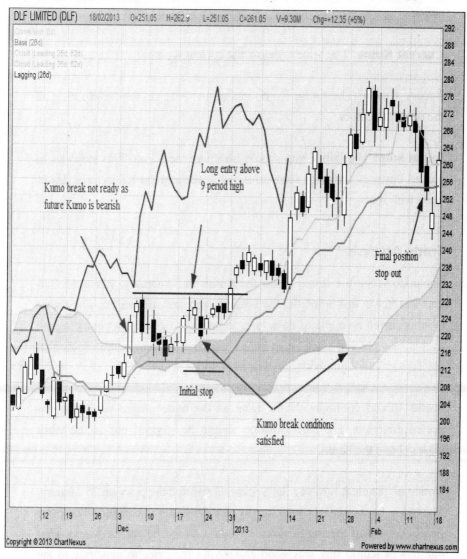

Figure 4.7: **Going long in DLF — note the Kumo break conditions being satisfied and the long entry and initial stop loss points**

Trade Set-up for Long Entry on 31 December

Tenkan / Kijun: The price is above both Tenkan and Kijun, which is bullish. Also, Tenkan is above the Kijun, which is also bullish.

Chikou: At the point of entry, the Chikou will be clear of any price interaction.

Current Kumo: Prices are above the current Kumo.

Future Kumo: The future Kumo is bullish, thus confirming all the other indicators.

Initial Stop: The initial stop will be below the Kijun. This stop can be moved up as the price moves higher and the Kijun trails upward with it.

Trade Analysis

The bullish Kumo break occurred on 5 December. However, the future Kumo was then still bearish, which should have stopped a trader from entering the trade. Prices then pulled back and took support on the Kijun. On 21 December, the future Kumo turned bullish and provided the green light for a long entry. Placing a buy order above the 9-period high, or above the 26-period high since the two highs were close together, would have got the trader in on 31 December. Notice that on this day, Senkou B was starting to go flat for the next few weeks. However, Tenkan was above the Kumo and close enough to the price to provide support for it.

Partial profits should be taken on a continuous basis as the price heads in the expected direction. Finally, the position should be stopped out as it closes below the Kijun.

Example 4.8: Short Trade Using the Kumo Break Strategy

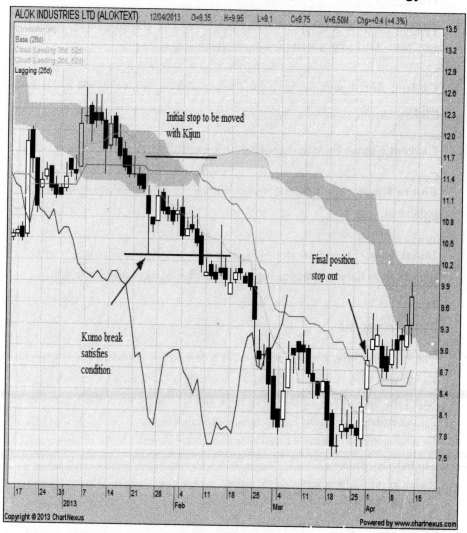

Figure 4.8: **Short trade in Alok Industries — the Kumo break and the initial stop are indicated**

Trade Set-up for Short Entry on 8 February

Tenkan / Kijun: The price is below both Tenkan and Kijun, which is a bearish sign. The Tenkan is below the Kijun, which is also bearish. And, both Tenkan and Kijun will continue to fall as the price goes lower.

Chikou: At the point of entry, the Chikou will be clear of any price interaction.

Current Kumo: Prices are below the current Kumo.

Future Kumo: The future Kumo is bearish, thus confirming all the other indicators.

Initial Stop: The initial stop will be above the Kijun. This stop can be moved down as the price starts to move lower and the Kijun trails with it.

Trade Analysis

The price closed below the Kumo on 24 January. At this point, Chikou was still trading in the price congestion of 26 days ago. It cleared this resistance in a couple of days and all the Ichimoku indicators were then lined up for a short entry below the 9-period low. For the purpose of getting the Kijun to also trend down, the entry level can be kept below the low of the candle which indicated the Kumo break.

Partials profits should be taken continuously as the trade progresses in the expected direction. Finally, the position should be fully stopped out when the stock closes above the Kijun.

Example 4.9: Going Short Using the Kumo Break Strategy

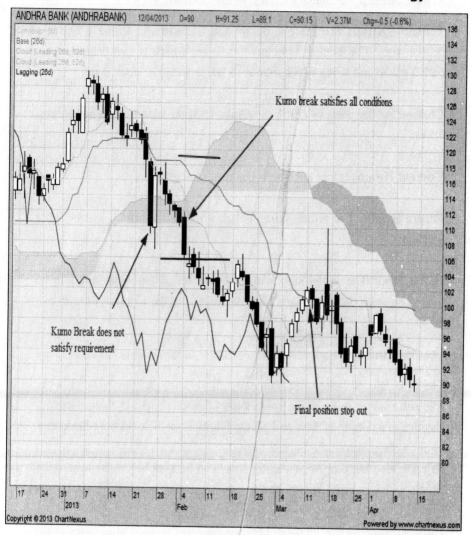

Figure 4.9: **Going short in Andhra Bank — the Kumo break is indicated in the chart**

Trade Set-up for Short Entry on 5 February

Tenkan / Kijun: The price is below both Tenkan and Kijun, which is a bearish sign. The Tenkan is below the Kijun, which is also bearish. And, both Tenkan and Kijun will continue to fall as price goes lower.

Chikou: At the point of entry, the Chikou will be clear of any price interaction.

Current Kumo: The price is below the current Kumo.

Future Kumo: The future Kumo is bearish, thus confirming all the other indicators.

Initial Stop: The initial stop will be above the Kijun. This stop can be moved down as the price starts to drop lower and the Kijun trails down with it.

Trade Analysis

When the price closed below the Kumo on 24 January, the future Kumo was still bullish. This was a caution that the trade should not be taken. Notice how the stock used the flat Senkou B as support. It rallied and was rejected at the Kijun. This time as the price came down, it ran out downward of the flat Senkou B. The Kumo started to go in a flux. Perfect timing for the bears! The price closed below the Kumo with a big bearish candle and the conditions for a short entry trade were satisfied on 5 February. A sell order below this candle would force the Tenkan and Kijun to also move down in the expected direction of the trade.

Partial profits should continuously be taken as the trade progresses in the expected direction. Finally, the entire position should be stopped out when the stock closes above the Kijun.

Example 4.10: Going Short with Kumo Break Strategy

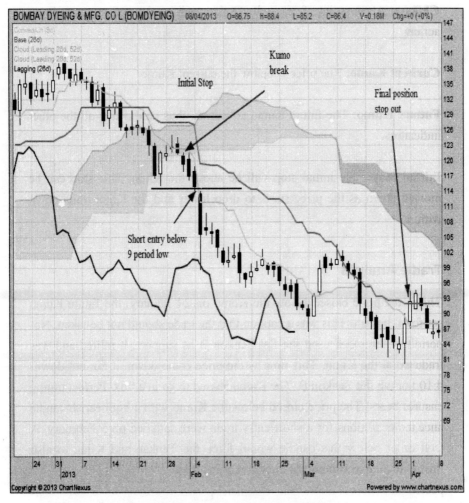

Figure 4.10: **Going short in Bombay Dyeing — note the Kumo break, the short entry and the initial stop points**

Trade Set-up for Short Entry on 4 February

Tenkan / Kijun: The price is below both Tenkan and Kijun, which is a bearish sign. The Tenkan is below the Kijun, which is also a bearish sign. And, both Tenkan and Kijun will continue to fall as price moves lower.

Chikou: At the point of entry, the Chikou will be clear of any price interaction.

Current Kumo: The price is below the current Kumo.

Future Kumo: The future Kumo is bearish, thus confirming all the other indicators.

Initial Stop: The initial stop will be above the Kijun. This stop can be moved down as the price starts to move lower and the Kijun trails down with it.

Trade Analysis

The price closed below the Kumo on 31 January. The future Kumo looked set for a bearish twist the next day. A short sell order placed below the 9-period low would not only bring the Tenkan down, but also the Kijun. The trade would have triggered on 4 February. Notice from the chart in Figure 4.10 that after 3 days, the 26-period highs would keep getting lower. This ensures that the Kijun would also head south to provide downside guidance to the stock.

Profits should continuously be taken as the trade progresses in the expected direction. Finally, the complete position should be stopped out when the stock closes above the Kijun.

Example 4.11: Going Short with Kumo Break Strategy

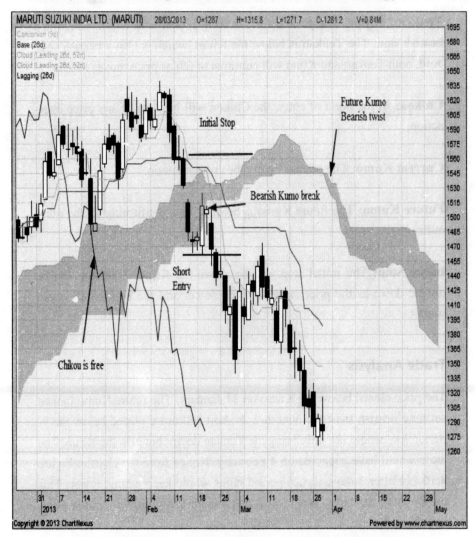

Figure 4.11: **Going short in Maruti Suzuki — the bearish Kumo break, the trade entry and initial stop loss points are indicated**

Trade Set-up for Short Entry on 21 February

Tenkan / Kijun: The price is below the Tenkan and Kijun, which is a bearish sign. The Tenkan is below the Kijun, which is also bearish. And, both Tenkan and Kijun will continue to fall as the price goes lower.

Chikou: At the point of entry, the Chikou will be clear of any price interaction.

Current Kumo: The price is below the current Kumo.

Future Kumo: The future Kumo turned bearish, thus confirming all the other indicators.

Initial Stop: The initial stop will be above the Kijun. This stop can be moved down as the price starts to head lower and the Kijun trails downward with it.

Trade Analysis

The price closed below the Kumo on 20 February. The future Kumo along with the Chikou and other Ichimoku requirements were thus satisfied for a short entry signal. A short sell order below the 9-period low would draw the Tenkan and Kijun down in the expected direction. Notice again the flat Senkou B where the price took support for a couple of days. Unfortunately for the bulls, though, the price ran out of this support area. Watch that flat Kumo!

Profits should continuously be taken as the trade progresses in the expected direction. Finally, the position should be entirely closed when the stock closes above the Kijun.

Example 4.12: Going Long Using the Kumo Break Strategy

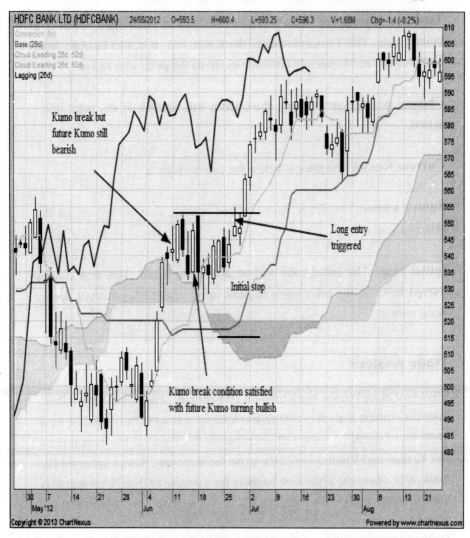

Figure 4.12: **Going long in HDFC Bank — note the bullish Kumo break, the entry and initial stop points**

Trade Set-up for Long Entry on 27 June

Tenkan / Kijun: The price is above the Tenkan and Kijun, which is a bullish sign. Tenkan is above the Kijun, which is also bullish. And, both Tenkan and Kijun will continue to rise as the price goes higher.

Chikou: At the point of entry, the Chikou will be clear of any price interaction.

Current Kumo: The price is above the current Kumo.

Future Kumo: The future Kumo is bullish, confirming all the other indicators.

Initial Stop: The initial stop will be below the Kijun. This stop can be moved up as the price starts to rise higher and the Kijun trails upward with it.

Trade Analysis

Price closed above the Kumo on 11 June. At this point, the Chikou was about to emerge from price congestion area and the future Kumo was still bearish. It was still a waiting game at this time. On 15 June, however, all the Ichimoku components lined up for a long entry above the 9-period high. This was triggered on 27 June. The Tenkan and Kijun were both drawn up when the trade was triggered as the 9-day high and 26-day high were the same. You will notice in the chart how the Kijun acts as support for the uptrending stock.

Profits should be taken continuously as the trade progresses in the expected direction. The entire position should be stopped out when the stock closes below the Kijun.

Example 4.13: Going Short Using the Kumo Break Strategy

Figure 4.13: **Going short in Bajaj Hindustan — note the Kumo break, the short entry and the initial stop points**

Trade Set-up for Short Entry on 12 November

Tenkan / Kijun: The price is below the Tenkan and Kijun, which is bearish. The Tenkan is below the Kijun, which is also bearish. And, both Tenkan and Kijun will continue to fall as the price goes lower.

Chikou: At the point of entry, the Chikou will be clear of any price interaction.

Current Kumo: The price is below the current Kumo.

Future Kumo: The future Kumo has turned bearish, effectively confirming all the other indicators.

Initial Stop: The initial stop will be above the Kijun. This stop can be moved down as the price starts to move lower and the Kijun trails downward with it.

Trade Analysis

As you can see in Figure 4.13, the price closed below the Kumo on October 30. All Ichimoku components were lined up for a short entry below the 9-period low. In this case it would be below the low of the candle that closed below the Kumo. What should one be aware of in this case? The flat Senkou B. We have seen specific examples of how this Kumo component influences price. It is a magnet for prices. The price rallies back to the flat Senkou B but fails at the Tenkan. The strongly trending Tenkan contains the price. You can see in Figure 4.13 how even in the days ahead the price tries to rally intraday towards the Kumo. By that time, however, even the Kijun is trending down, adding to the downward pressure on price.

Profits should continuously be taken as the trade progresses in the expected direction. Finally, the position should be entirely stopped out when the stock closes above the Kijun.

Example 4.14: Going Short Using the Kumo Break Strategy

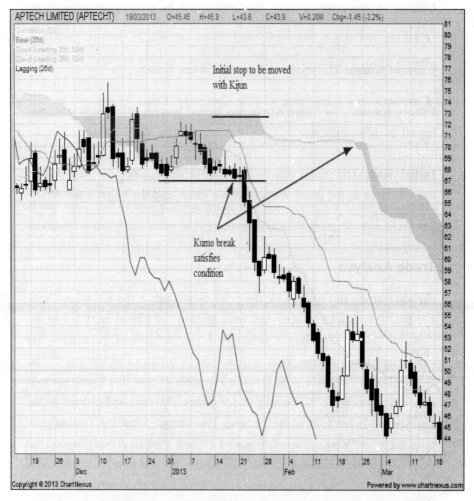

Figure 4.14: **Going short in Aptech Limited — the Kumo break and the initial stop points are indicated**

Trade Set-up for Short Entry on 22 January

Tenkan / Kijun: In the chart in Figure 4.14, the price is below Tenkan and Kijun, which is a bearish sign. Tenkan is below the Kijun, which is also bearish. And, both Tenkan and Kijun will continue to fall as the price goes lower.

Chikou: At the point of entry, the Chikou will be clear of any price interaction.

Current Kumo: The price is below the current Kumo.

Future Kumo: The future Kumo turned bearish, thus confirming all the other indicators.

Initial Stop: The initial stop will be above the Kijun. This stop can be moved lower as the price starts to move down and the Kijun trails downward with it.

Trade Analysis

In Figure 4.14, the price closed below the Kumo on 10 January. The future Kumo, however, was still bullish. When this future Kumo turned bearish, a sell order placed below the 9-period low would have got a trader in a short position on 22 January. The Tenkan and Kijun both drew lower with the trade entry.

Notice, too, the earlier Kumo break in December. By now, the reader would know the reason why this Kumo break was not a sell signal — because the Chikou was still in price congestion. The Chikou has to be in an open space for a trend to continue and develop momentum.

Partial profits should continuously be taken as the trade progresses in the expected direction. Finally, the entire position should be stopped out when the stock closes above the Kijun.

Example 4.15: Going Long — and Short — Using the Kumo Break Strategy

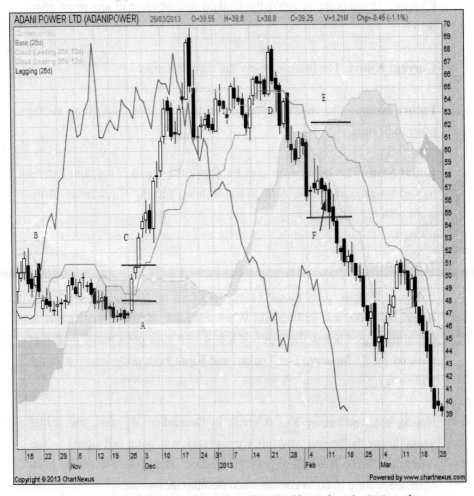

Figure 4.15: **Going long and short using the Kumo break strategy in Adani Power**

Trade Set-up for Long Entry in Adani Power on 30 November

Tenkan / Kijun: In the chart in Figure 4.15, the price is above the Tenkan and Kijun, which is a bullish sign. The Tenkan is above the Kijun, which is also bullish. And, both Tenkan and Kijun will continue to rise as the price climbs higher.

Chikou: At the point of entry, the Chikou will be clear of any price interaction (Point B).

Current Kumo: Prices are above the current Kumo.

Future Kumo: The future Kumo is bullish, thus confirming all the other indicators.

Initial Stop: The initial stop will be below the Kijun (Point A). This stop can be moved up as prices start to rise and the Kijun follows suit.

Trade Analysis

The price had closed above the Kumo on 27 November. The Chikou then was, however, still in price congestion from 26 days ago. From the chart, traders can visually note that it would take another day for Chikou to be free of the congestion. As the price closed higher the next day, it cleared the Chikou and thus aligned all Ichimoku components for a long entry (Point C) above the 9-period high. Note again in this chart how the flat Senkou B provided support for the stock from where it rallied to close above the Kumo.

Profits should continuously be taken as the trade progresses in the expected direction. Finally, the position should be entirely stopped out as the stock closes below the Kijun.

Trade Set-up for Short Entry in Adani Power on 12 February

Tenkan / Kijun: Staying with Figure 4.15, we find that the price is below the Tenkan and Kijun, which is bearish. The Tenkan is below the Kijun a which is also bearish. And both Tenkan and Kijun will continue to fall as the price heads lower.

Chikou: As can be seen from the chart, Chikou will be clear of any price interaction at the point of entry (Point D).

Current Kumo: Prices are below the current Kumo.

Future Kumo: The future Kumo turned bearish, thus confirming all the other indicators.

Initial Stop: The initial stop will be above the Kijun (Point E). This stop can be moved lower as the price starts to move lower and the Kijun trails down with it.

Trade Analysis

As Figure 4.15 reveals, the price closed below the Kumo on 2 February. The Chikou was free at this point, but the future Kumo was still bullish. The price tries to rally as it is attracted to the flat Senkou B. At this point, Tenkan is, however, strongly heading down to offer resistance and guide the price lower. As the future Kumo gets the bearish twist, a sell order placed below the 9-period low would trigger a short entry for a very profitable trade (Point F).

Profits should continuously be taken as the trade progresses in the expected direction. Final position should be stopped out when the stock closes above the Kijun.

Example 4.16: Long Trade Using the Kumo Break Strategy

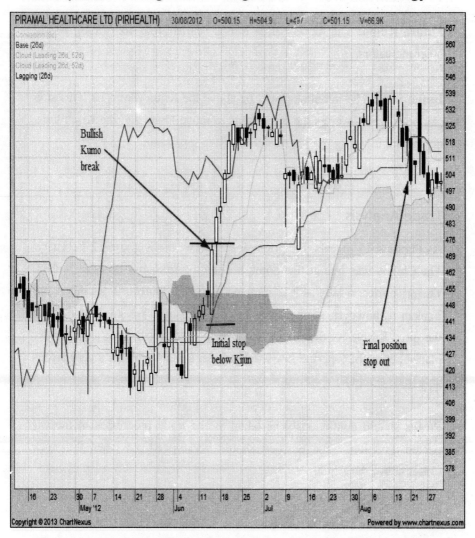

Figure 4.16: **Going long in Piramal Healthcare — the bullish Kumo break, the initial stop and the final stop positions are indicated**

Trade Set-up for Long Entry on 15 June

Tenkan / Kijun: As can be seen in the chart in Figure 4.16, the price is above the Tenkan and Kijun, which is a bullish sign. Tenkan is above the Kijun, which is also bullish. And, both Tenkan and Kijun will continue to rise as the price goes higher.

Chikou: At the point of trade entry, the Chikou will be clear of any price interaction.

Current Kumo: Prices are above the current Kumo.

Future Kumo: The future Kumo is bullish, thus confirming all the other indicators.

Initial Stop: The initial stop will be below the Kijun. This stop can be moved higher as the price starts to move up and the Kijun trails higher with it.

Trade Analysis

The price closed above the Kumo on 14 June with a strong bullish candle. This was needed as the price was contending with a flat Kumo (Senkou B). A weak close above this would likely have drawn the price back inside the Kumo, thus leading to a false breakout. This strong candle pulled the Tenkan and Kijun up with it. At this point all Ichimoku components were lined up for a long entry above the 9-period high. This would have triggered the next day as bulls came back and pierced the previous day's high.

Partial Profits should be taken along the way as the stock rises as anticipated.

Example 4.17: Going Short Using the Kumo Break Strategy

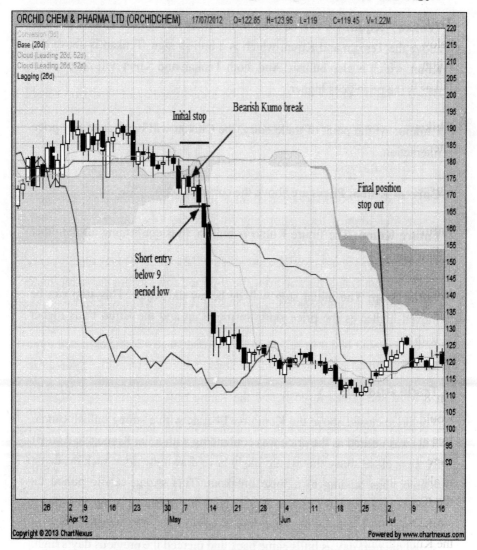

Figure 4.17: **Going short in Orchid Chem & Pharma — note the bearish Kumo break, the entry, the initial and final stop points**

Trade Set-up for Short Entry on 10 May

Tenkan / Kijun: As the chart in Figure 4.17 would confirm, the price is below the Tenkan and Kijun, which is a bearish sign. Tenkan is below the Kijun, which is also bearish. And, both Tenkan and Kijun will continue to fall as the price heads lower.

Chikou: At the point of trade entry, the Chikou will be clear of any price interaction.

Current Kumo: Prices are below the current Kumo.

Future Kumo: The future Kumo is bearish, thus confirming all the other indicators.

Initial Stop: The initial stop will be above the Kijun. This stop can be moved lower as prices start to head down.

Trade Analysis

On 8 May, the price closed below the Kumo. Zooming in on the chart would probably indicate a Kumo break on 6 May, but the Chikou was not free at that point, thus nullifying any trade entry. All Ichimoku components were lined up for a short entry below the 9-period low, which in this case is also be the 26-period low. Notice in the chart how the price waited for the Kumo to thin out. The thicker Kumo in the days prior supported the stock, but the bulls could not capitalize on this. Bears then took control as the Kumo thinned. As informed traders piled up on the short side, the price collapsed, yielding a handsome profit in a short period of time.

Example 4.18: Long Trade Using the Kumo Break Strategy

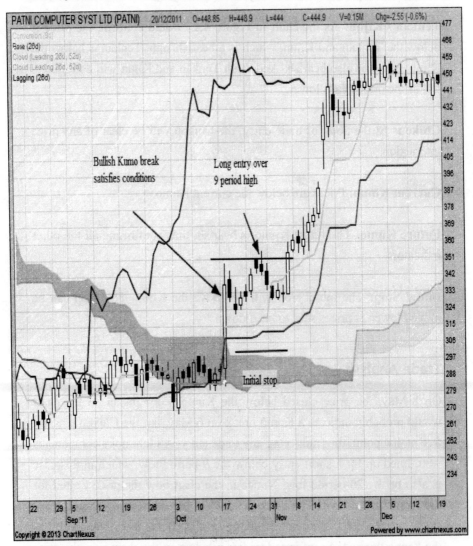

Figure 4.18: **Going long in Patni Computer — note the Kumo break, the long entry and initial stop points**

Trade Set-up for Long Entry on 28 October

Tenkan / Kijun: As you would note from the chart in Figure 4.18, the price is above the Tenkan and Kijun, which is a bullish sign. Tenkan is above the Kijun, which is also bullish. The Tenkan and Kijun will continue to rise as the price goes higher.

Chikou: At the point of trade entry, the Chikou will be clear of any price interaction.

Current Kumo: The price is above the current Kumo.

Future Kumo: The future Kumo is bullish, thus confirming all the other indicators.

Initial Stop: The initial stop will be below the Kijun. This stop can be moved up as the price starts to rise higher and the Kijun follows it upward.

Trade Analysis

The price closed above the Kumo on 18 October with a strong bullish candle. Notice how the candle found the end of the flat Kumo (Senkou B) to break through and closed above it. This bullish move was large enough to move the Tenkan and Kijun above the Kumo. All Ichimoku components were then lined up for a trade entry above the 9-period high, which would also be the 26 period high. The trade entry would have triggered on 28 October. The price moved up nicely, following the bullish breakout.

Partial profits should be taken along the way as the stock rises as anticipated, and the position should be fully exited below the Kijun.

Example 4.19: Short Trade Using the Kumo Break Strategy

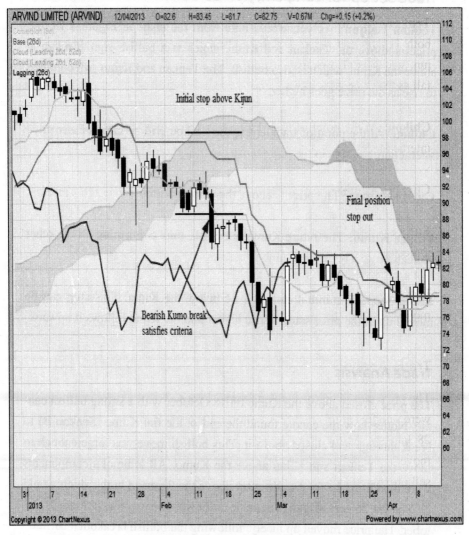

Figure 4.19: **Short trade in Arvind Ltd. — the bearish Kumo break and the initial and final stops are indicated**

Trade Set-up for Short Entry on 14 February

Tenkan / Kijun: As the chart in Figure 4.19 reveals, the price is below both Tenkan and Kijun, which is a bearish sign. Tenkan is below the Kijun, which is also bearish. And, both Tenkan and Kijun will continue to fall as the price goes lower.

Chikou: At the point of trade entry, the Chikou will be clear of any price interaction.

Current Kumo: Prices are below the current Kumo.

Future Kumo: The future Kumo is bearish, thus confirming all the other indicators.

Initial Stop: The initial stop will be above the Kijun. This stop can be moved down as the price starts to move lower.

Trade Analysis

The price closed below the Kumo on 7 February. All Ichimoku conditions were satisfied at this point for a short trade entry below the 9-period low of 28 January. As the price wavered for the next few days, the 9-period low moved up and the trade would have executed as shown in Figure 4.19. The sell order could still have been kept at the same price as that of 28 January and would have triggered on 14 February.

Partial profits should be taken along the way as the price moves in the anticipated direction and the trade position should be finally closed when the price closes above the Kijun.

When the Kumo Break Strategy Fails

Let us now look at a few examples of a failed Kumo break strategy.

Example 4.20: Failed Long Using the Kumo Break Strategy

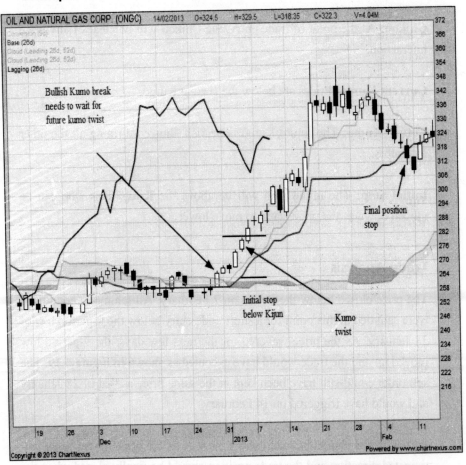

Figure 4.20: **Going long using the Kumo break strategy in ONGC and losing**

Trade Set-up for Long Entry on 4 January

Tenkan / Kijun: As you would notice in the chart of ONGC in Figure 4.20, the price is above Tenkan and Kijun, which is a bullish sign. Tenkan is above the Kijun, which is also bullish. And, both Tenkan and Kijun will continue to rise as the price goes higher.

Chikou: At the point of entry, the Chikou will be clear of any price interaction.

Current Kumo: Prices are above the current Kumo.

Future Kumo: The future Kumo is bullish, thus confirming all the other indicators.

Initial Stop: The initial stop will be below the Kijun. This stop can be moved up as prices start to move higher and Kijun trails with it.

Trade Analysis

The price closed above the Kumo on 28 December. To enter a long trade, one would need to wait for the future Kumo to turn bullish. This happened on 3 January. A buy stop order placed above the 3 January candle would draw the Tenkan as well as Kijun up.

As the stock moves up, profits should be taken off the table and the position should be completely exited when the price closes below the Kijun on 8 February.

Example 4.21: Failed Long Trade Using the Kumo Break Strategy

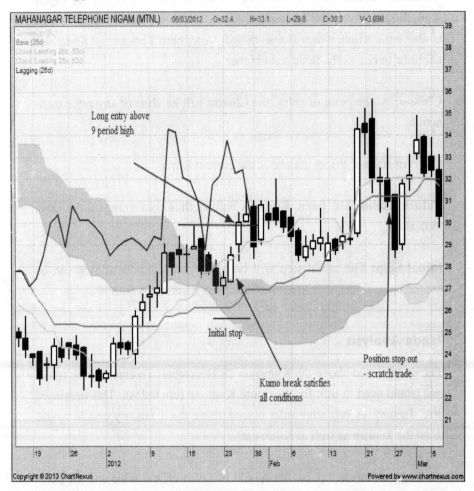

Figure 4.21: **Going long using the Kumo break strategy in MTNL and losing**

Trade Set-up for Long Entry on 25 January

Tenkan / Kijun: As can be seen in the chart in Figure 4.21, the price is above the Tenkan and Kijun, which is a bullish sign. Also, the Tenkan is above the Kijun, which too is bullish. And, both Tenkan and Kijun will continue to rise as the price goes higher.

Chikou: At the point of entry, the Chikou will be clear of any price interaction.

Current Kumo: Prices are above the current Kumo.

Future Kumo: The future Kumo is bullish, thus confirming all the other indicators.

Initial Stop: The initial stop will be below the Kijun. This stop can be moved up as prices start to move higher and Kijun trails upward with it.

Trade Analysis

MTNL's price closed above the Kumo on 24 January. All Ichimoku components were thus aligned for a long entry. A buy order placed above the preceding 9-period high was the correct entry setup. This would have executed the following day. On 24 February, the price closed decisively below the Kijun and the trader would need to abort the trade and get out at that point.

As mentioned all along in the previous examples, profit should always be taken on a continuous basis as the trade progresses along the expected path. If no profits were taken, then this would have resulted in a scratch trade.

There were a couple of days — 14 and 16 February for example — when the price closed just below the Kijun. But this was not decisive at all. In such cases, I would recommend getting stopped out the next day if the price moves below the low of the candle which closed below the Kijun.

Example 4.22: Failed Short Trade Using the Kumo Break Strategy

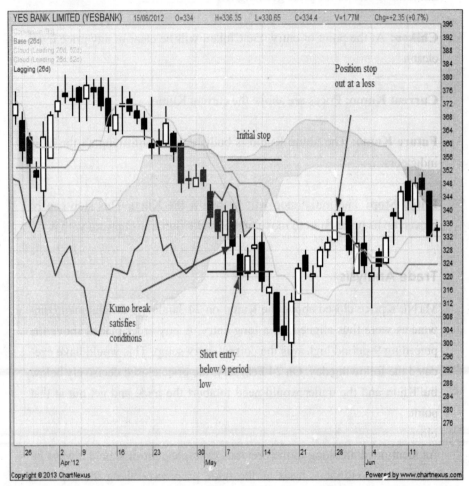

Figure 4.22: **Failing with the Kumo break strategy in Yes Bank**

Trade Set-up for Short Entry on 9 May

Tenkan / Kijun: The chart in Figure 4.22 reveals that the price is below the Tenkan and Kijun, which is a bearish sign. The Tenkan is below the

Kijun, which is also bearish. And, both Tenkan and Kijun will continue to fall as the price goes lower.

Chikou: As can be seen in the chart in Figure 4.21, the Chikou will be clear of any price interaction at the point of entry.

Current Kumo: Prices are below the current Kumo.

Future Kumo: The future Kumo is bearish, thus confirming all the other indicators.

Initial Stop: The initial stop will be placed above the Kijun. This stop can be moved lower as prices start to move down.

Trade Analysis

The price closed below the Kumo on 8 May. All Ichimoku components were therefore aligned for a short entry. A sell order placed below the 9-period low was the correct entry setup. This would have executed the next day and the stock promptly followed the Tenkan down for a few days. A bullish engulfing candlestick signal stopped the fall and the price then started reversing. The trade would have stopped out on 28 May as the price closed above the Kijun. This would have resulted in a losing trade, assuming no profits were taken along the downward move.

Notice, however, that loss is small compared to the big profits that one makes when the stock starts trending. This is the basis of successful trading . . . small losses and larger profits.

Example 4.23: Failed Short Trade Using the Kumo Break Strategy

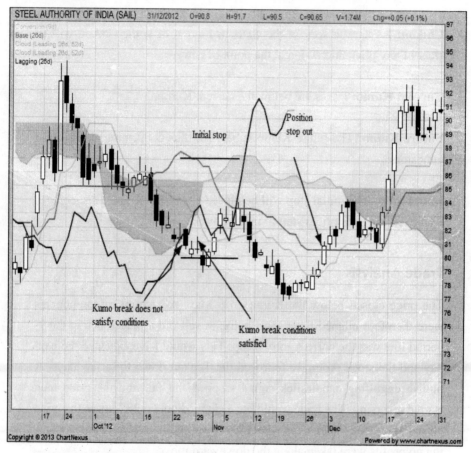

Figure 4.23: **Unprofitable short trade using the Kumo break strategy in SAIL**

Trade Set-up for Short Entry on 30 October

Tenkan / Kijun: As can be seen in the chart in Figure 4.22, the price is below the Tenkan and Kijun, which is a bearish sign. The Tenkan is below Kijun, which is also bearish. And, both Tenkan and Kijun will continue to fall as the price heads lower.

Chikou: At the point of entry, the Chikou will be clear of any price interaction.

Current Kumo: Prices are below the current Kumo.

Future Kumo: The future Kumo is bearish, confirming all the other indicators.

Initial Stop: The initial stop will be above the Kijun. This stop can be moved lower as prices start to move down.

Trade Analysis

On 25 October, the price closed below the Kumo. At this point, the future Kumo was still bullish, thus not satisfying the short entry criteria. The bearish future Kumo twist occurred on 29 October and the short entry could then be placed below the 9-period low. Notice that once the trade was executed the next day, the stock rallied and failed at the Kijun. It then had a nice move down. However, the price then reversed again without handing the trader a good point to take profits. The trade would have stopped out on November 30. Again, notice, that the loss one would have incurred here was only a small one.

~

Traders need always to keep in mind that nothing is guaranteed in trading. What you are doing by using Ichimoku is that you are putting probabilities in your favor. This also means that sometimes the trades will not go as expected. It is then best to cut one's loss as soon as the reason for entering the trade is negated. Many traders act like deer paralyzed by a headlight. The consequences are also the same — the market will trample you. To become a successful trader, you will have to accept losses as a part of your bigger strategy.

5

Tenkan / Kijun Cross Strategy

This is my favourite Ichimoku strategy.

Basic Strategy

- Long positions are initiated when the Tenkan crosses the Kijun to the upside.

- Short positions are initiated when the Tenkan crosses the Kijun to the downside.

Rules / Conditions

Price *versus* Current Kumo

In Chapter 4, we looked at the different bullish and bearish scenarios related to the T/K cross *versus* current Kumo. Personally, I tend to give this less importance. As long as all the other Ichimoku components are lined up, I consider the T/K cross a good entry signal. However, when the price is either below or in the Kumo, the trader needs to be careful about Senkou

B. If Senkou B is observed to be currently flat, and remains flat in the near future, the trade needs to be evaluated thoroughly before putting in a buy / sell order. Keep in mind that a flat Senkou B will have the tendency to offer resistance to the stock. So the price will more than likely reverse at Senkou B if the Kijun and Tenkan aren't close by to provide support in the anticipated direction. As one studies more and more charts, these dynamics of support and resistance will become clearer.

On a long entry below the Kumo, it will favor the trade if the Kumo is thin. Chances then are that the price will burst through it. This is also true for a thin Kumo which is in a flux.

When the Kumo is fat, price will expend a lot of energy simply going through it. This needs to be considered in the trade and the target formalized accordingly.

Future Kumo

- If one is looking at a long entry with the T/K cross, the future Kumo needs to be bullish.
- If it is a short entry, then the future Kumo needs to be bearish.

In the long entry, it helps more if both Senkou A and Senkou B are pointing in the upward direction. For the short entry, it is better for both Senkou A and Senkou B to be pointing south.

Many times, though, for the long side, Senkou A will be pointing upwards and Senkou B will be flat. On the short side, Senkou A will be pointing down and Senkou B will be flat.

Keep in mind that the T/K cross is signaling a possible trend reversal. As the trend develops, it will pull Senkou B with it at some point in time.

Chikou

Repeating that the Chikou is critical for trading success with Ichimoku will only help in emphasizing its importance.

The T/K strategy, like the Kumo break strategy, needs the Chikou to be free and clear.

There will be many opportunities where the trader sees the T/K cross and is tempted to buy even as he observes that the Chikou is mired in price action of 26 periods ago. Heed this warning and do not take those trades. They are the low probability trades. Find stocks with the T/K cross and a free Chikou to enter and profit from. The Ichimoku system makes it visually easy to see when the Chikou will be free if it currently isn't. One can the anticipate the chart conditions at that point in time. Remember, everything revolves around 9, 26 and 52.

Tenkan and Kijun

Since we are trading the T/K cross, Tenkan will be above the Kijun for a long entry and below the Kijun for a short entry.

Sometimes when the T/K cross sets up, the other components might not yet be aligned. However, the price might keep pushing in your expected direction. It is a better strategy not to chase price, but wait for a pullback. Price will often come back to equilibrium (Kijun) and then climb back up over the Tenkan. By this time, more often than not, the other Ichimoku components will be aligned for the trade.

Price *versus* the Tenkan and Kijun

- For a long entry, the price should be above the Tenkan and Kijun.
- For a short entry, the price should be below the Tenkan and Kijun.

Keep in mind that you should not enter a trade if the price is considerably stretched away from the Tenkan and Kijun. The latter two are magnets and, in most cases, will attract the price back towards themselves. This is especially so in cases where a big jump in price causes a T/K cross. You will then see that the Kijun soon goes flat and pulls the price towards it. Entering a trade when price is near the Tenkan and Kijun has the advantage of a lower stop loss setting.

Trade Entry

Once all the Ichimoku components signal a long trade entry, a buy order can be put in above the highest high of the last 9 periods. Correspondingly, for a short entry, a sell order can be programmed below the lowest low of the prior 9 periods. This assures the trader that price will draw the Tenkan with it.

Initial Stop Loss

It is a good idea to put the initial stop loss under the Kijun. As the trend progresses in the anticipated direction, the Kijun will follow and the stop can be trailed with it. Profits should always be taken on a continuous basis as they build up. Finally, the entire position should be exited when the price closes below the Kijun.

T/K Cross Trading Strategy in Action

The next several charts show the T/K trading strategy in action. I have described the scenarios in the initial few charts and then for the rest, I have hit on the key indicators that need to be looked at.

Also, do pay attention to the charts showing losing trades. Even with all Ichimoku components lining up, there will be times when the trade fails. That is an inevitable part of the game.

Example 5.1: Going Short Using the T/K Cross Strategy

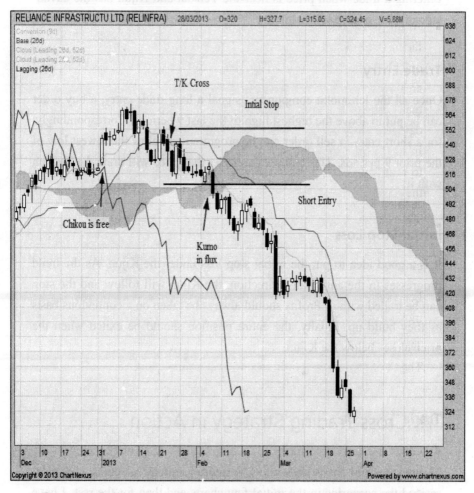

Figure 5.1: **Going short in Reliance Infrastructure — the T/K cross and the short trade entry are indicated on the chart**

Trade Set-up

- Our first entry criterion for going short using the Tenkan / Kijun cross is satisfied on 24 January.

- Notice in Figure 5.1 that on this date the Chikou is getting support from the candles of 26 days ago, namely the candle of 18 December.

- At this point, one can visually see in Figure 5.1 that the Chikou will be facing congestion for the next 7 to 8 days unless the stock drops quickly through the support offered by those candles in the congestion area. Keep in mind that you do not want to get in until the Chikou is actually free of that congestion. It is possible that during the next 7 to 8 days, the stock drops intraday but comes back up by the end of the day. In such a case, the Chikou will still be in the congestion area. You need to wait for a closing candle to visually see the Chikou closing clear of the support area.

- After the T/K cross, the stock rallies and fails to close decisively over the Kijun. This is expected by the trader. If the stock had managed to close above the Kijun, the trade scenario is voided.

- For the next few days, the stock drops giving the Tenkan time to start moving down and the Chikou to become free of price congestion.

- The Kumo is in flux. This is perfect for a cross of the price below it. The future Kumo is almost turning over to bearish.

Trade Analysis

- Given the current scenario, the trader can place a sell-stop entry at the lows as indicated in Figure 5.1. Setting the entry below the lows would do two things. One, it would draw the Tenkan down and, two, it would also draw the Kijun down. Keep in mind that you want these two components to help guide the stock lower. A looking at the chart suggests that the Tenkan would be moving down anyway as the highs over the last 9 days continue to fall. The Kijun would start moving down after the next 7 days as the 26-week highs start dropping down. So you are assured that the resistance lines will shortly be moving in your favor.

- The initial stop out point would be above the Kijun. As the stock moves lower, the Kijun will follow, and the stop can be trailed with it.

- Currently, the stock still should be held short (or long put options). Profits must be taken along the way. Rest of the position should be closed when the stock closes above the Kijun.

Example 5.2: Going Short Using the T/K Cross Strategy

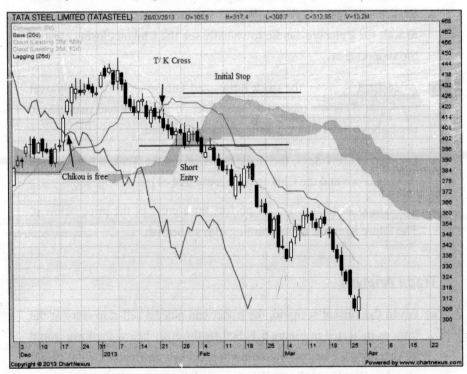

Figure 5.2: **Going short in Tata Steel — the bearish T/K cross and trade entry points are indicated on the chart**

Trade Analysis for Short Entry on 4 February

- Our short entry criteria of the T/K cross was satisfied on 22 January (*see* Figure 5.2).

- At that point, the Chikou was still above the corresponding price 26 days ago. It needed to cross the price to the downside. This happened on 25 January.

- The Kumo is in flux, which will make it easier for the price to cross and close below it. Notice that the Senkou B does support the price for 4 days before Tenkan provides enough resistance for a break. This would be the ideal entry point for the short entry.

- At the entry point, the future Kumo looks set to turn bearish in the next few days, thus confirming the rest of the Ichimoku components. Can you guess why the future twist is inevitable? Hint: Look at the prior 52-day lows. They are rising, which will make Senkou B go higher. Senkou A will go lower when Tenkan / Kijun more downward at the buy point, leading to the future Kumo twist.

- The initial stop out point would be above the Kijun, as indicated in Figure 5.2.

- At this entry point, the Kijun would also be drawn down as it is the lowest point of the last 26 days. Also notice that the Kijun will move down in the next 4 to 5 days as the highs of the last 26 days start dropping down. This should provide continued downward pressure for the stock. It will also help in moving the stop out point lower and reducing the loss in case the trade does not go as expected.

- The short position can continue to be held till the end of the period covered in Figure 5.2, with partial profits taken along the way. The remaining position should be closed when the stock closes above the Kijun.

- Notice how the stock was able to break the thin and trending Kumo on 4 February. A few more days of consolidation would have provided strong support for the stock in the form of a flat Senkou B. It would have been harder at that point for the Tenkan to offer resistance, especially with the Kijun being some distance away. Not that this doesn't happen, but it is difficult and a scenario best avoided to be traded until the stock closes below the Kumo.

Example 5.3: Going Long Using the T/K Cross Strategy

Figure 5.3: **Going long in TCS — the bullish T/K cross, the trade entry and initial stop points are indicated on the chart**

Trade Set-up for Long Entry on 14 January

Tenkan / Kijun: In Figure 5.3 the price is above both Tenkan and Kijun, which is bullish. Tenkan is above the Kijun, which is also bullish. The T/K cross, however, occurred within the Kumo, which is considered neutral. The Tenkan and Kijun will continue to rise as the price climbs higher.

Chikou: At the point of entry, Chikou will be clear of any price interaction (*see* Figure 5.3). This is bullish as there is no near term resistance.

Current Kumo: The current Kumo is bullish. Rising prices will also bring the Kijun and Tenkan above the Kumo.

Future Kumo: The future Kumo has turned bullish, confirming all the other indicators.

Initial Stop: The initial stop will be below the Kijun, as indicated in Figure 5.3. Keep in mind that the Kijun represents equilibrium. This stop can be moved up as price starts to rise and draws the Kijun up with it.

Trade Analysis

Notice that in Figure 5.3 the point of entry comes after one of the most powerful candlestick signals, namely a Kicker signal. This should add to the confidence of the trader that this trade has a very high probability of success. Profits should be taken along the way and the entire position should finally be stopped out when price closes below the Kijun.

Another entry point would have been near 6 February. All conditions at this point were bullish as well and the reader can mentally make a note of all the different Ichimoku components to confirm this.

Example 5.4: Going Short Using the T/K Cross Strategy

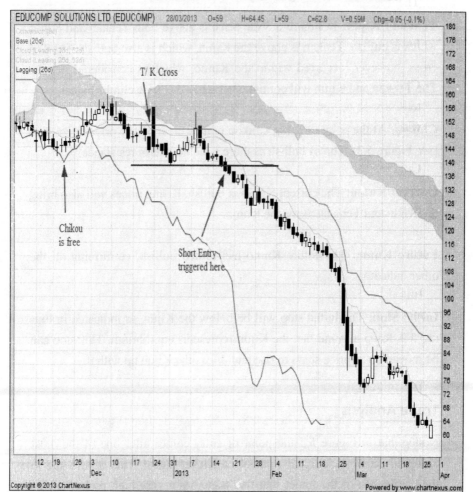

Figure 5.4: **Going short in Educomp — the bearish T/K cross and trade entry point are indicated on the chart. Note that the Chikou is free**

Trade Set-up for Short Entry on 17 January

Tenkan / Kijun: In Figure 5.4, the price is below both Tenkan and Kijun, which is a bearish sign. Tenkan is below the Kijun, which is also bearish.

The T/K cross occurred below the Kumo, which is considered strongly bearish. Both Tenkan and Kijun will continue to fall as the price goes lower, offering resistance to the stock.

Chikou: As indicated in Figure 5.4, Chikou will be clear of any price interaction at the point of entry,. This should help the price move down without much support coming in.

Current Kumo: The current Kumo is bearish.

Future Kumo: The future Kumo is also bearish, confirming all the other indicators. Notice this section is strongly trending down as both Senkou A and Senkou B are being drawn downward.

Initial Stop: The initial stop will be above the Kijun. This stop can be moved down as the price starts to head lower and draws the Kijun down with itself.

Trade Analysis

The trader could have initiated the trade anytime after 9 January. However getting in on the 17th at the price level then prevailing assured the trader that the stock would draw the Kijun and Tenkan down with itself. Also, this will clear the support area that the Chikou created due to the candle from 31 December. So much confirmation adds a lot to the probabilities in the traders favor.

Partial profits should be taken at various points as the stock moves down and the remaining position should be finally stopped out when price closes below the Kijun.

Example 5.5: Going Long Using the T/K Cross Strategy

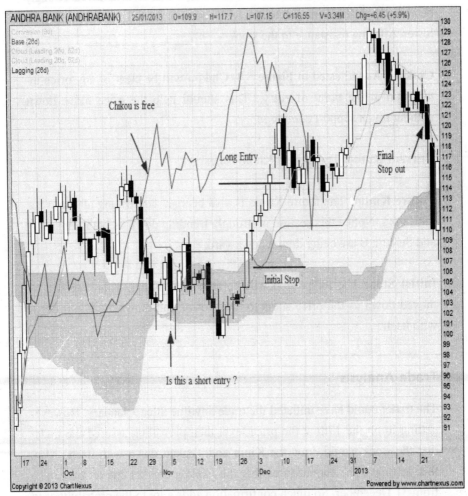

Figure 5.5: **Going long in Andhra Bank using the T/K cross strategy -- note the long entry and initial stop loss points on the chart**

Trade Set-up for Long Entry on 6 December

Tenkan / Kijun: In Figure 5.5, the price is above both Tenkan and Kijun, which is bullish. Tenkan is above the Kijun, which is also a bullish sign.

The T/K cross occurred within the Kumo, something which is considered neutral. Both Tenkan and Kijun will continue to rise as the price goes up, offering support to the stock.

Chikou: As can be seen in Figure 5.5, the Chikou will be clear of any price interaction at the point of entry. This should help the price move up without much resistance coming in.

Current Kumo: The current Kumo is bullish.

Future Kumo: The future Kumo is also bullish confirming all the other indicators. You would notice that the future Kumo is trending up as the 52-day low rises higher and the Tenkan / Kijun also trend higher.

Initial Stop: The initial stop will be below the Kijun. This stop can be moved up as the price starts to rise higher and draw the Kijun up with itself.

Trade Analysis

Notice how throughout the chart in Figure 5.5 the flat Kijun and the flat Senkou B provide support / resistance to the stock. Remember, the Kijun is the 26-period equilibrium and Senkou B is the 52-period equilibrium. If the price gets too far away from a flat Kijun, a pullback will most likely occur to bring things to base again.

Partial profits should be taken as the stock moves up and the entire remaining position would be finally stopped out on 23 January when the price closes below the Kijun.

Example 5.6: Going Long — and Short — Using the T/K Cross Strategy

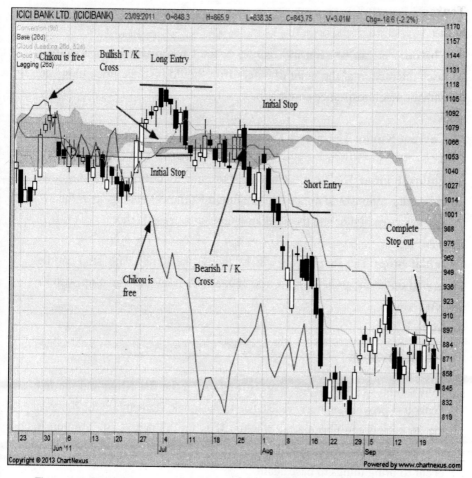

Figure 5.6: **Going long — and going short — in ICICI Bank. The T/K crosses, entry points and initial stops are indicated on the chart**

The chart in Figure 5.6 depicts two trading opportunities. Let us analyze each separately.

Trade Set-up for Long Entry on 2 July

Tenkan / Kijun: The price is above both Tenkan and Kijun, which is a bullish sign. Tenkan is above the Kijun — see the "Bullish T/K cross" on the chart in Figure 5.6 — which is also bullish. The T/K cross occurred within the Kumo, something which is considered neutral. The Tenkan and Kijun will continue to rise as the price goes up, thus offering support to the stock.

Chikou: As can be seen in Figure 5.6, the Chikou will be clear of any price interaction at the point of entry. This should help the price move down without much support coming in.

Current Kumo: The current Kumo is bearish.

Future Kumo: The future Kumo is also bearish but will turn bullish in the next couple of days. This is due to the fact that the Tenkan will rise as the 9-period lows get higher in the next few days.

Initial Stop: The initial stop will be below the Kijun (*see* Figure 5.6). This stop can be moved up as prices start to move higher.

Trade Analysis

This is one of those scenarios mentioned in the Chapter 2, where the price runs away from the Kijun. The Tenkan keeps up and supports the price, but the Kijun, which is the equilibrium, goes flat. In this case notice where the low of the previous 26 days is on June 21, which is close to the current price action. This means there will be another couple of weeks before the Kijun starts moving higher on its own. The way it stands now, the Kijun can move up only if the stock price goes higher every day. As stated earlier, these trades should be taken with caution, preferably with reduced position sizes. In this case, the trade would not have been executed as the buy point was not breached.

Trade Set-up for Short Entry on 3 August

Tenkan / Kijun: As can be seen in Figure 5.6, in early August the price is below both Tenkan and Kijun, which is a bearish sign. Tenkan is below the Kijun, which is also bearish. The T/K cross occurred within the Kumo, something which is considered neutral. At the point of entry, the Tenkan and Kijun will continue to fall as price goes lower, offering resistance to the stock.

Chikou: At the point of short entry, the Chikou will be clear of any price interaction (*see* Figure 5.6). This should help the price move down without much support coming in.

Current Kumo: The current Kumo is bearish.

Future Kumo: The future Kumo is also bearish, thus confirming all the other indicators.

Initial Stop: Figure 5.6 indicates the initial stop above the Kijun. This stop can be moved down as price starts to move lower and draws the Kijun down with itself.

Trade Analysis

All the conditions were met on 2 August for a short entry the day after. Should the trader buy below the low of that day or, as shown on the chart, below the low of the candle on 29 July? The idea of the current entry is to get the Tenkan and Kijun to move lower with the price to help keep guiding it down. If you short below the low of the 2 August candle, the Tenkan / Kijun pair would not necessarily move down. This can happen only if the price goes down through the low of the candle of 29 July. Notice also that within the next 5 days, the Kijun will start moving down on its own because the 26-day high will start dropping. So the trader is assured at this point that the equilibrium is going to be much lower in the coming days even if the stock does not move down fast.

This is a very important concept worth emphasizing time and time again — as a trader, you want the equilibrium to be heading in the direction you are trading. This not only provides constant resistance to the stock, but also helps you lock in more profits every day you are in the trade.

Example 5.7: Going Short Using the T/K Cross Strategy

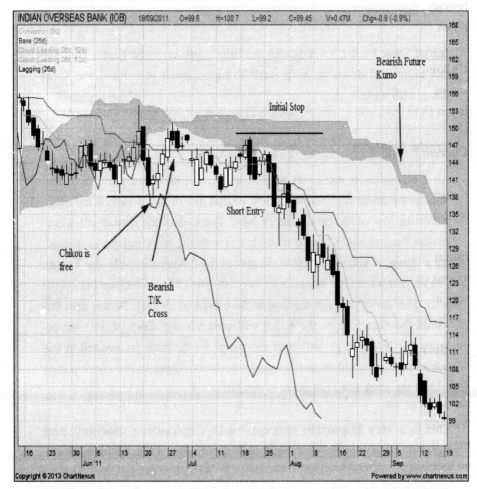

Figure 5.7: **Going short in Indian Overseas Bank — the bearish T/K cross, the free Chikou, the trade entry point and the initial stop loss are indicated on the chart**

Trade Set-up for Short Entry on 28 July

Tenkan / Kijun: The price is below both Tenkan and Kijun, which is a bearish sign. Tenkan is below the Kijun, which is also bearish. The T/K cross occurred below the Kumo, something which is considered strongly bearish. Both Tenkan and Kijun will continue to drop as the stock goes down.

Chikou: At the point of entry, the Chikou will be clear of any price inter-action. This should help the price move down without much support coming in from the buyers.

Current Kumo: The current Kumo is bearish.

Future Kumo: The future Kumo is also bearish, confirming all the other indicators.

Initial Stop: The initial stop will be above the Kijun. This stop can be moved down as the price starts to head lower and draws the Kijun down with it.

Trade Analysis

In this example there was a considerable lag between the T/K cross and the short entry point. What was the main reason for this delay? The Chikou was still wavering in the congestion zone of the price action during this time. It was clear on 28 July at the entry price point, that the Chikou would no longer face immediate resistance.

You can also see in Figure 5.7 that four days after the entry, the Kijun would drop down because the 26-period high would drop. This would move the equilibrium price down, which is the desired goal of the short trade. Also notice how the Kijun provided resistance to the stock as it rallied two days after the entry point. Depending on the direction of approach, the flat Kijun offer an excellent resistance / support level for the stock.

Profits should be taken continuously as the stock moves down. The entire position can finally be stopped out once the price closes above the Kijun.

Example 5.8: Going Long Using the T/K Cross Strategy

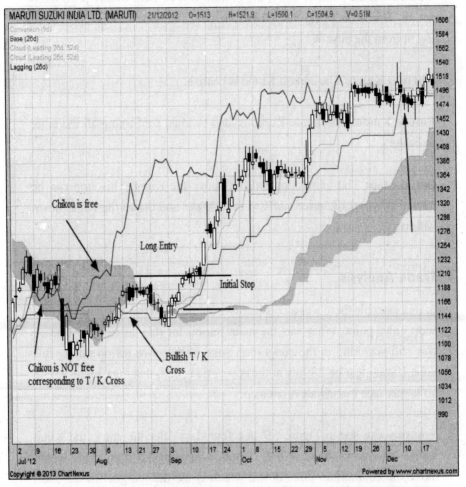

Figure 5.8: **Going long in Maruti — the bullish T/K cross, the long entry point and the initial stop loss are indicated on the chart**

Trade Set-up for Long Entry on 8 September

Tenkan / Kijun: In the chart in Figure 5.8 the price is above both Tenkan and Kijun, which is a bullish sign. Tenkan is above the Kijun, which is also bullish. The T/K cross occurred below the Kumo, something which is considered weak bullish. The Tenkan and Kijun will continue to rise as the stock goes up.

Chikou: As shown in Figure 5.8, the Chikou will be clear of any price interaction at the point of entry. This should help the price moving up without much resistance.

Current Kumo: The current Kumo is bearish, but very thin.

Future Kumo: The future Kumo is bullish and rising, indicating a possible trend in progress.

Initial Stop: The initial stop will be below the Kijun. This stop can be moved up as prices start to move higher and draw the Kijun up.

Trade Analysis

The first thing to notice in Figure 5.8 is that when the T/K cross occurred, the Chikou was not free. Not only was it below the price, it was also bumping against it. Thus, it had no room to run, so to speak. In other words, as the current price was rising and approaching the prices from 26 days ago, the traders who had bought the stock then were selling out. They were getting out of the stock and providing the additional supply; not good if you are long.

As the bulls gave up, prices fell back and got attracted to the flat Kijun, the equilibrium. The next horde of bulls drove the price back up. This time around, the Chikou was free. There was not much additional supply of the stock. Buying above the high of 22 August assured the trader of both a rising Tenkan and a rising Kijun. A rising Kijun and Tenkan would get Senkou-A heading in the upward direction, too. Notice that the Kijun would get additional upward pressure as the 26-period low begins to climb.

Profits should be taken along the way as the price rockets up. The entire remaining position should finally be stopped out once the stock closes below the Kijun.

Example 5.9: Going Long Using the T/K Cross Strategy

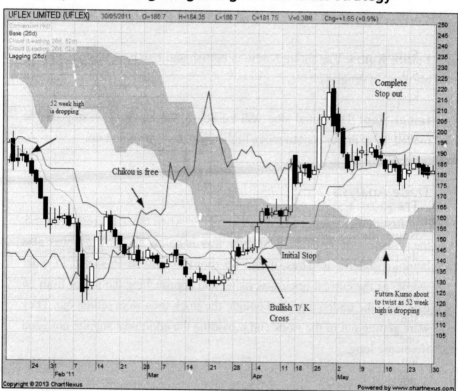

Figure 5.9: **Going long in Uflex — the bullish T/K cross and initial stop loss points are indicated on the chart**

Trade Set-up for Long Entry on 5 April

Tenkan / Kijun: The price is above both Tenkan and Kijun, which is a bullish sign. Tenkan is above the Kijun, which is also bullish. The T/K cross occurred below the Kumo, which is considered weak bullish (*see* Figure 5.9). The Tenkan and Kijun will continue to rise as the stock goes up.

Chikou: As Figure 5.9 shows, the Chikou will be clear of any price inter-action at the point of entry. This should help the price move up without much resistance.

Current Kumo: Price is above the current Kumo.

Future Kumo: The future Kumo is also bearish but as indicated in Figure 5.9, a twist is possible in the next couple of days as the 52-period high keeps dropping.

Initial Stop: The initial stop will be below the Kijun. This stop can be moved up as the price starts to move higher and draws the Kijun up with it.

Trade Analysis

Notice that on the day of entry, the Tenkan is in a position to move up as the prior 9-period lows keep getting higher. So the stock will get supported by the Tenkan even if the price moves a little sideways. The Kijun, on the other hand, will have to wait for a few weeks before the 26-period lows start climbing. This is definitely not an ideal scenario, but still a bullish one. Also keep in mind that price will have to contend with a flat Kumo top. The flat Senkou B often provides resistance to a rising stock. If the stock fails at that point and closes below the Tenkan, one can expect the price to come back to the flat Kijun equilibrium. This scenario should not be ignored in such situations.

In this case there is a clear level where the first profits should be taken. If one knows that a flat Kumo will provide resistance, shouldn't one use that level to take some of the profits off the table? After the stock breaks above that level and continues moving up, one can keep taking partial profits along the way. Finally, the entire position should be stopped out when the stock closes below the Kijun.

Example 5.10: Going Long Using the T/K Cross Strategy

Figure 5.10: **Going long in Unitech — the bullish T/K cross, the free Chikou, long trade entry point and the initial stop loss are indicated on the chart**

Trade Set-up for Long Entry on 29 November

Tenkan / Kijun: The price is above both Tenkan and Kijun, which is a bullish sign. Tenkan is above the Kijun, which is also bullish. The T/K cross occurred above the Kumo (*see* Figure 5.10), which is considered strongly bullish. The Tenkan and Kijun will continue to rise as the stock goes up.

Chikou: As you can see in Figure 5.10, the Chikou will be clear of any price interaction at the point of entry. This should help the price move up without much resistance.

Current Kumo: The current Kumo is bullish.

Future Kumo: The future Kumo is also bullish.

Initial Stop: The initial stop will be below the Kijun. This stop can be raised once the price starts to move higher and draws the Kijun up with it.

Trade Analysis

As can be seen in Figure 5.10, at the time of the T/K cross the stock closed below the Kijun but immediately bounced back up. Remember that the flat Kijun acts like a magnet. Once price closed back above the Tenkan, the trade still could not be initiated because of the Chikou not being free. The big bullish candle of November 28 brought the Chikou in open-sky territory. All the trader needs to do at this point is to set a buy stop at the high of the candle and get into the trade.

Partial profits should periodically be taken along the way as the price increases. The entire position should finally be stopped out once the stock closes below the Kijun.

Example 5.11: Going Short Using the T/K Cross Strategy

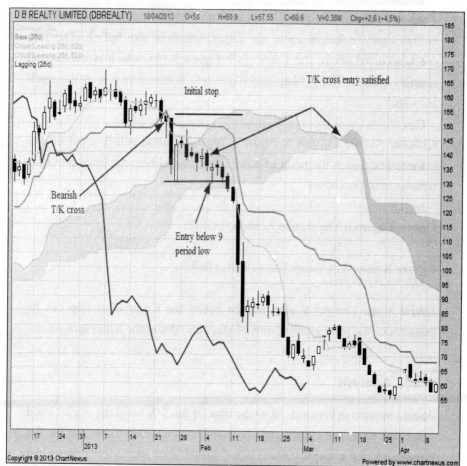

Figure 5.11: **Going short in DB Realty — the bearish T/K cross, the trade entry and the initial stop points are indicated**

Trade Set-up for Short Entry on 5 February

Tenkan / Kijun: The price is below both Tenkan and Kijun, which is a bearish sign. Tenkan is below the Kijun, which is also bearish. As you would note in Figure 5.11, the T/K cross occurred above the Kumo, which is considered weak bearish.

Chikou: At the point of entry, the Chikou will be clear of any price interaction. This should help the price move down without much resistance.

Current Kumo: Price is consolidating in the Kumo.

Future Kumo: The future Kumo has turned bearish one day ago.

Initial Stop: The initial stop will be above the Kijun. This stop can be moved down as the price starts to move lower.

Trade Analysis

At the point of the T/K cross, the Chikou is not free. A day after the cross, the stock drops hard and the Chikou crosses the price action from 26 days ago. However, the future Kumo is still bullish. Also note that price has now run away from the Tenkan and Kijun. At this point, the trader can wait for the conditions to set up for a short entry. As the future Kumo turns bearish, the trader can put in a sell order below the 9-period low, as indicated in Figure 5.11. This ensures that Tenkan will be drawn down to guide the stock. In this case, the 9-period low is also the 26-period low. This means the Kijun will be drawn down as well. The trader does need to be cautious in the next couple of days as the current Kumo is flat beneath the stock and could provide support. However, in this case the stock is near the edge of the flat Senkou B and finds that point to break down. (It's amazing at how often this scenario occurs).

Profits should periodically be taken along the way as the price plummets following the Kumo break.

Example 5.12: Going Long Using the T/K Cross Strategy

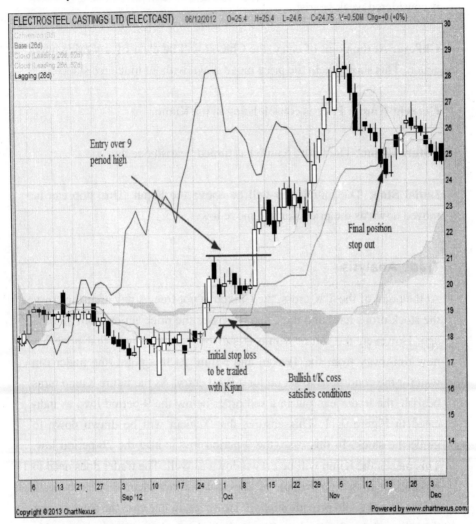

Figure 5.12: **Going long in Electrosteel Casting — the bullish T/K cross, the long trade entry and the initial stop loss points are indicated on the chart**

Trade Set-up for Long Entry on 11 October

Tenkan / Kijun: The price is above both Tenkan and Kijun, which is a bullish sign. Tenkan is above the Kijun, which is also bullish. The T/K cross occurred above the Kumo, which is considered strongly bullish. Both Tenkan and Kijun will continue to rise as the stock goes up.

Chikou: At the point of entry, the Chikou will be clear of any price interaction. This should help the price move up without much resistance.

Current Kumo: Price is above the current Kumo.

Future Kumo: The future Kumo is bullish.

Initial Stop: The initial stop will be below the Kijun. This stop can be moved up as the price starts to move higher and draws the Kijun up with it.

Trade Analysis

Chikou became free of the price action when the stock rallied towards the end of September. However, the T/K cross happened a few days later to give the long entry signal. At this point, the trader should set the buy entry above the 9-period high. In this case, the 26-period high matches the 9-period high. Keeping the buy point above this price assures the trader that Tenkan and Kijun will move in the anticipated direction.

Profits should be taken along the way as the price rises. The entire position should finally be stopped out below the Kijun.

Example 5.13: Going Long Using the T/K Cross Strategy

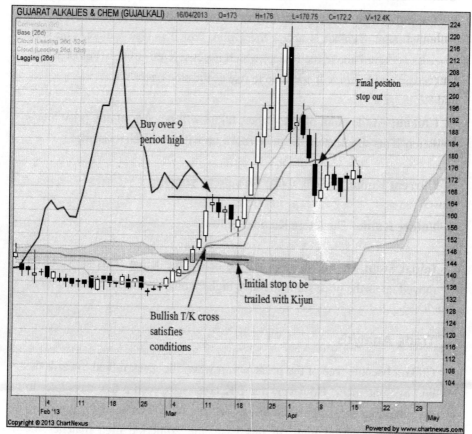

Figure 5.13: **Going long in Gujarat Alkalies — note the bullish T/K cross, trade entry and initial stop loss points using the T/K cross strategy**

Trade Set-up for Long Entry on 12 March

Tenkan / Kijun: In the chart in Figure 5.13, the price is above both Tenkan and Kijun, which is a bullish sign. Tenkan is above the Kijun, which is also bullish. The T/K cross occurred above the Kumo, which is considered strongly bullish. Both Tenkan and Kijun will continue to rise as the stock price goes up.

Chikou: As you can see in Figure 5.13, the Chikou will be clear of any price interaction at the point of entry. This should help the price move up without much resistance.

Current Kumo: The current Kumo is bearish, but the price, the Tenkan and Kijun are above it.

Future Kumo: The future Kumo is bullish and rising.

Initial Stop: The initial stop will be below the Kijun. This stop can be moved up as the price starts to move higher and draws the Kijun up along with it.

Trade Analysis

The Ichimoku components were all aligned at the point of entry. While the price was a little distant from the Tenkan and Kijun, but notice in Figure 5.13 that the Tenkan would be moving up every day for the next 9 days as the 9-period lows keep moving higher. Another alternative entry point would have been on 20 March as the price broke above the 9-period high again. This time, the Kijun was moving up as well which provided added confidence in the trade.

This chart highlights perfectly why one needs to take profits on a continuous basis as the price moves in the anticipated direction. After hitting a peak at ₹ 222, the price fell to around ₹ 170, where the trade would have stopped out. That is a lot of profit wasted. It is imperative to follow good money management technique to capture profits on a regular basis. Only the final portion of the position should be the one to get stopped out below the Kijun if the trade has run in your favor.

Example 5.14: Going Short Using the T/K Cross Strategy

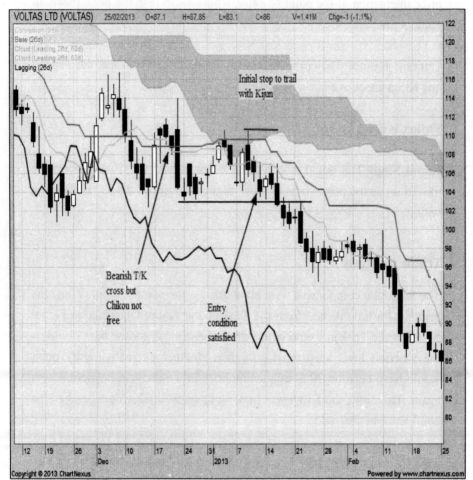

Figure 5.14: **Going short in Voltas — the bearish T/K cross, entry and initial stop loss point are indicated on the chart**

Trade Set-up for Short Entry on 16 January

Tenkan / Kijun: In Figure 5.14, the price is below both Tenkan and Kijun, which is bearish. Tenkan is below the Kijun, which is also bearish.

The T/K cross occurred below the Kumo, which is considered strongly bearish. The Tenkan and Kijun will continue to fall as the stock price drops.

Chikou: As you can see in the chart in Figure 5.14, the Chikou will be clear of any price interaction at the point of entry. This should help the price move down without much resistance.

Current Kumo: The current Kumo is bearish and the price, the Tenkan and the Kijun are below it.

Future Kumo: The future Kumo is bearish.

Initial Stop: The initial stop will be above the Kijun. This stop can be moved lower as the price starts to head down.

Trade Analysis

The bearish T/K cross occurred on 20 December. At that point, the Chikou was not free as it would bump to the price in the next couple of days in case the price stagnated. The stock rallied back to test the flat Kijun and twice failed to close above it. The trader can get ready to go short when price closed back below the Tenkan on 9 January. Placing a sell stop below the 9-period low will work. However, note that there is only a slight difference between the 9-period low and the 26-period low. Why not then set the stop below the 26-period low! This way the trader is assured that the Kijun (equilibrium) also moves down along with the Tenkan.

As always, partial profits should be regularly taken as the price moves in the expected direction.

Example 5.15: Going Short Using the T/K Cross Strategy

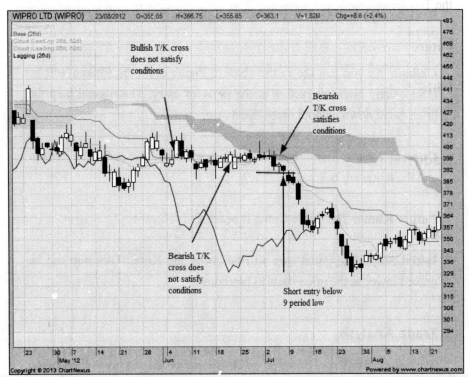

Figure 5.15: **Going short in Wipro — the bearish T/K cross and the trade entry points are indicated on the chart**

Trade Set-up for Short Entry on 6 July

Tenkan/ Kijun: In the chart in Figure 5.15, the price is below both Tenkan and Kijun, which is a bearish sign. Tenkan is below the Kijun, which is also bearish. The T/K cross occurred below the Kumo, which is considered strongly bearish.

Chikou: It's shown in Figure 5.15 that the Chikou will be clear of any price interaction at the point of entry. This should help the price move down without much resistance.

Current Kumo: The current Kumo is bearish in Figure 5.15 and the price, the Tenkan and the Kijun are below it.

Future Kumo: The future Kumo is also bearish.

Initial Stop: The initial stop will be above the Kijun. This stop can be lowered as the price starts to move down.

Trade Analysis

The bearish T/K cross occurred on 5 July. All the Ichimoku components were then aligned for a short entry below the 9-period low. This would assure that Tenkan moves down with the stock price. It would also be a good idea to get in below the low of June 12 candle. This is the 26-period low and not much distant from the 9-period low. In this case, the trader pays a little insurance premium to ensure that the Kijun also moves in the anticipated direction to provide downside guidance to the stock. Partial profits should be taken regularly as the price moves in the expected direction. The final position should be closed out either when the price closes above the Kijun, or once it goes through the stop level above the Kijun.

You will notice in the chart in Figure 5.15 that there are two more T/K crosses marked. It is pretty obvious why they do not satisfy the entry criteria. The first T/K cross, which is bullish, occurred on 6 June. What was the position of the Chikou then? The Chikou was trading in the congestion price area. This in itself negates any potential trade. Besides this, the future Kumo cloud was also bearish.

The second T/K cross occurred on 22 June. This was a bearish cross below the Kumo, a potentially strong shorting signal. However, there were two components which flashed a red signal to the trade. Look at the chart and analyze it before reading further.

In Figure 5.15, the Chikou is above the price action from 26 days ago. If the price goes down, it could find support on the candles. That is why we need the Chikou to be below price action, in open territory. The second component which is not aligned is the price itself. The price is above both Kijun and Tenkan. For a bearish trade, the price should be below the Tenkan and Kijun.

Example 5.16: Going Long Using the T/K Cross Strategy

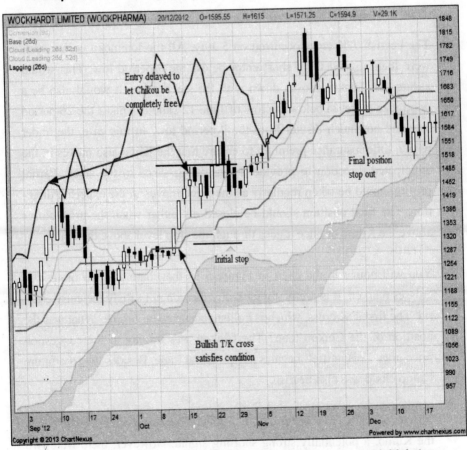

Figure 5.16: **Going long in Wockhardt Ltd. — the T/K cross and initial stop loss points are also indicated**

Trade Set-up for Long Entry on 23 October

Tenkan / Kijun: In Figure 5.16, the price is above both Tenkan and Kijun, which is bullish. Tenkan is above the Kijun, which is also bullish. The T/K cross occurred above the Kumo, which is considered strongly bullish. The Tenkan and Kijun will continue to rise as the stock price goes up.

Chikou: As can be seen in Figure 5.16, the Chikou will be clear of any price interaction at the point of entry. This should help the price move up without much resistance.

Current Kumo: The current Kumo is bullish, and the price, the Tenkan and the Kijun are above the price.

Future Kumo: The future Kumo is bullish and rising.

Initial Stop: The initial stop will be below the Kijun. This stop can be moved up as the price starts to move higher and draws the Kijun up with itself.

Trade Analysis

The T/K cross occurred on 12 October. At this time all Ichimoku components were aligned for a long entry. Notice, however, that the Chikou, even though above the price action from 26 days ago, clearly had the potential to bump into price action were the current price to stagnate for a couple of days. That interaction with price congestion could cause things to change and negate the bullish nature of the chart. In such cases it is best to wait a few days to ensure that the Chikou will be free. As soon as the trader sees that the Chikou will be in open skies, the trade can be entered above the 9-period high. In this case, the 9-period high would also be the 26-period high. Both Tenkan and Kijun will move up if the trade is triggered.

Partial profits should be taken on a continuous basis as the stock rises and the entire remaining position should be stopped out below the Kijun.

Example 5.17: Going Short Using the T/K Cross Strategy

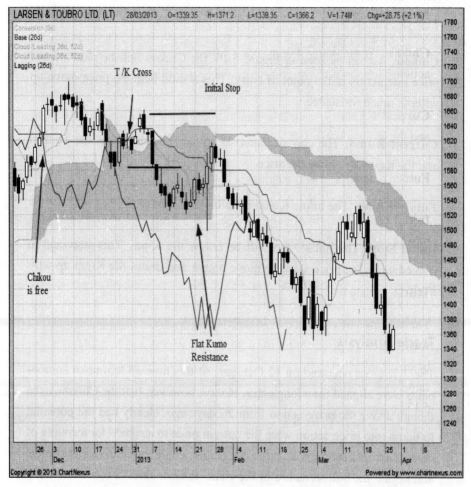

Figure 5.17: **Going short in Larsen & Toubro — the T/K cross and initial stops are indicated on the chart**

Trade Set-up for Short Entry on 8 January

Tenkan / Kijun: In the chart in Figure 5.17, the price is below both Tenkan and Kijun, which is a bearish sign. Tenkan is below the Kijun, which is also bearish. The T/K cross occurred above the Kumo, which is a weak bearish signal.

Chikou: At the point of entry, the Chikou will be clear of any price interaction. This should help the price move down without much resistance.

Current Kumo: The current Kumo is bullish and the price, the Tenkan and the Kijun are inside it.

Future Kumo: The future Kumo is bearish.

Initial Stop: The initial stop will be above the Kijun. This stop can be moved lower as prices start to fall.

Trade Analysis

The bearish T/K cross occurred on 31 December. At that time, the Chikou was still above price action from 26 days ago. Then on 7 January, the big bearish candle led to the price closing below the Tenkan and Kijun. At the same time, it cleared the Chikou of resistance. As can be seen in Figure 5.17, a short entry below the 9-period low can be initiated at this point.

What does the trader need to be careful of in this chart? The obvious flat Senkou B!

This should alert the trader to take some profits off the table near the flat Kumo. The remaining portion would have been stopped out above the Kijun on 25 January. One strategy would be to completely close out the position at an obvious resistance point like in this case. The flat Senkou B would be the target of the trade and the entire position liquidated as soon as the target is hit.

Example 5.18: Going Long Using the T/K Cross Strategy

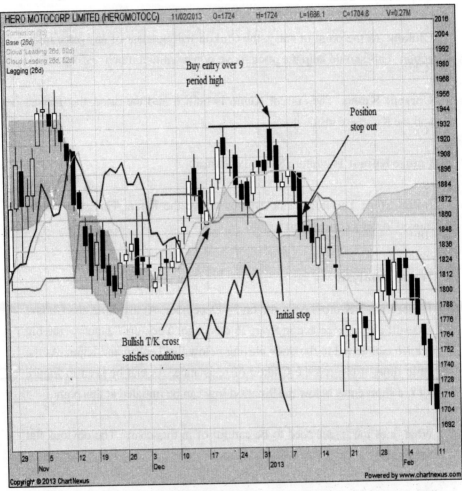

Figure 5.18: **Going long in Hero Motocorp — the bullish T/K cross, the entry and initial stop loss points are indicated**

Trade Set-up for Long Entry on 2 January

Tenkan / Kijun: In Figure 5.18, the price is above the Tenkan and Kijun, which is a bullish sign. Tenkan is above the Kijun, which is also bullish. The T/K cross occurred above the Kumo, which is considered strongly bullish. And the Tenkan and Kijun will continue to rise as the stock price goes up.

Chikou: At the point of entry, the Chikou will be clear of any price interaction. This should help the price move up without much resistance.

Current Kumo: The current Kumo is bullish, and the price, the Tenkan and the Kijun are above it.

Future Kumo: The future Kumo is bullish.

Initial Stop: The initial stop will be below the Kijun. This stop can be moved up as prices start to rise higher and draw the Kijun up.

Trade Analysis

The T/K cross occurred on 19 December. At this point, the Chikou was still a day away from getting out of the price congestion area. The next day's candle aligned all the Ichimoku components for a buy entry above the 9-period high. This entry was triggered on 2 January. What happened next is an integral part of trading . . . a stop out with a loss! Do all trades work? No. Cutting your losses short and letting your profits run is the recipe for trading success.

Example 5.19: Going Long Using the T/K Cross Strategy

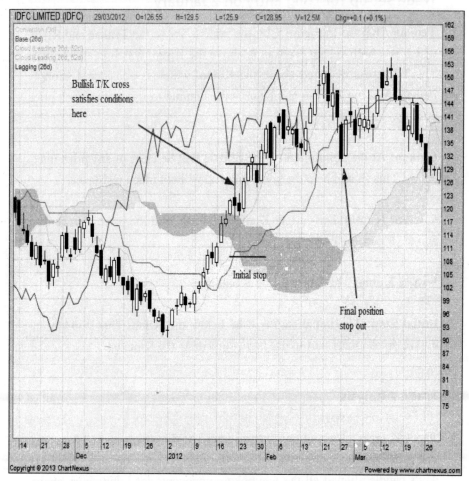

Figure 5.19: **Going long in IDFC — the bullish T/K cross and the initial stop are indicated on the chart**

Trade Set-up for Long Entry on 27 January

Tenkan / Kijun: The price is above both Tenkan and Kijun, which is a bullish sign. Tenkan is above the Kijun, which is also bullish. As can be seen in Figure 5.19, the T/K cross occurred below the Kumo, something which is considered weak bullish. The Tenkan and Kijun will continue to rise as the stock moves up.

Chikou: At the point of entry, the Chikou will be clear of any price interaction. This should help the price move up without much resistance.

Current Kumo: The current Kumo is bearish. The price and Tenkan are above it, but the Kijun is still within the Kumo cloud.

Future Kumo: The future Kumo is bullish.

Initial Stop: The initial stop will be below the Kijun. This stop can be moved up as the price starts to trend higher and draws the Kijun up with it.

Trade Analysis

The T/K cross occurred on 12 January. At this point, the Chikou was still below the price action of 26 days ago and the future Kumo was bearish. This meant that the bullish trade could not be initiated. The Chikou became free on 17 January. The long candle formation on 20 January pulled the Tenkan and Kijun up, which in turn caused Senkou A to cross Senkou B to the upside. At this point, setting a buy order above this candle's high would be the right strategy to enter the trade.

As the trade progresses in the expected direction, partial profits should be taken continuously and the final position would be fully stopped out on 27 February as the candle closes below the Kijun.

You will notice in the chart in Figure 5.19 that the day where the price broke above the flat Kumo. Isn't it interesting that the Kumo was running out of this strong flat attractive force, which helped the price to rally? The situation could have been completely changed had the Senkou B been flat for the next several days as the price was trying to break free of the Kumo.

Example 5.20: Going Short Using the T/K Cross Strategy

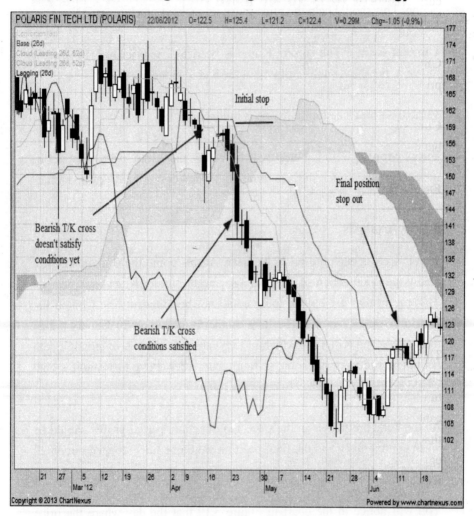

Figure 5.20: **Going short in Polaris — the bearish T/K cross and initial stop are indicated on the chart**

Trade Set-up for Short Entry on 25 April

Tenkan/ Kijun: The price is below both Tenkan and Kijun, which is bearish. Tenkan is below the Kijun, which is also bearish. The T/K cross occurred above the Kumo, which is considered a weak bearish sign. The Tenkan and Kijun will continue to fall as the stock price goes down.

Chikou: As can be seen in Figure 5.20, the Chikou will be clear of any price interaction at the point of entry.

Current Kumo: The current Kumo is bullish. Price is below the Kumo, but the Tenkan and Kijun are still within the cloud.

Future Kumo: The future Kumo is bearish.

Initial Stop: The initial stop will be above the Kijun. This stop can be moved down as the price starts to drop lower and draws the Kijun down with it.

Trade Analysis

The bearish T/K cross occurred on 13 April. A few days later, Chikou cleared the price congestion. However, one would need to wait for the future Kumo to turn bearish. This occurred on 24 April with the big bearish candle closing below the Kumo. The conditions for short entry were met at this point. A sell order below this candle's low would be the correct strategy to enter the trade. Entering the trade in this way would ensure that the Kijun and Tenkan are pulled down to guide the stock lower. Notice also in Figure 5.20 how the price used the portion of Kumo flux to break down. If the bears had tried knocking the price down a couple of weeks earlier, the flat Senkou B would have provided support for the price and the bulls could have rallied off from there.

As the stock moves lower, the initial stop would be trailed down with the Kijun. Partial profits should be taken along the way and the final position should be fully stopped out as the price closes above the Kijun.

Example 5.21: Going Long Using the T/K Cross Strategy

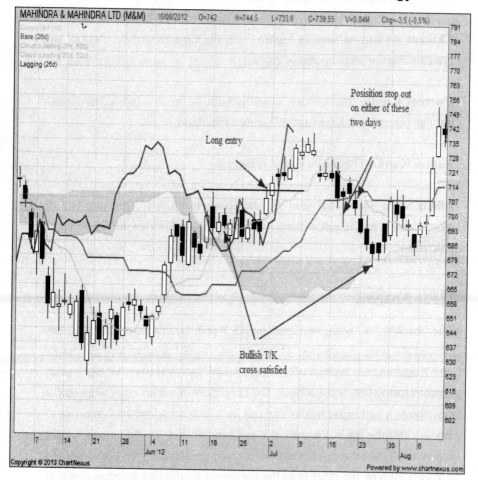

Figure 5.21: **Going long in Mahindra & Mahindra — the bullish T/K cross and the entry point are indicated on the chart**

Trade Set-up for Long Entry on 29 June

Tenkan / Kijun: The price is above both Tenkan and Kijun, which is a bullish sign. Tenkan is above the Kijun, which is also bullish. In Figure 5.21, the T/K cross occurred below the Kumo, which is considered a weak bullish sign. The Tenkan and Kijun will continue to rise as the stock price goes up.

Chikou: At the point of entry, the Chikou will be clear of any price interaction. This should help the price move up without much resistance.

Current Kumo: The current Kumo is bearish. Both the price and Tenkan are above it, but the Kijun is still within the cloud.

Future Kumo: The future Kumo is bullish.

Initial Stop: The initial stop will be below the Kijun. This stop can be moved up as the price starts to rise higher and draws the Kijun up with it.

Trade Analysis

As can be seen in Figure 5.21, the bullish T/K cross occurred on 8 June. A week later, Chikou cleared the price congestion from 26 periods ago. The future Kumo had a bullish twist on 20 June, thus setting the stage for a long trade entry. A stop above the 9-period high would ensure that Tenkan would move up in support of the price action. The stop would have triggered on 29 June. Even though the 9-period high had dropped lower on 29 June, it would still be in the trader's interest to keep the buy stop order at the original point. The difference is minimal, but the advantage gained in terms of ensuring that the Kijun rises with the trade is huge.

This trade would most probably have resulted in a loss. But the loss would be small compared to the profits generated by winning trades in a trader's portfolio.

Example 5.22: Going Long Using the T/K Cross Strategy

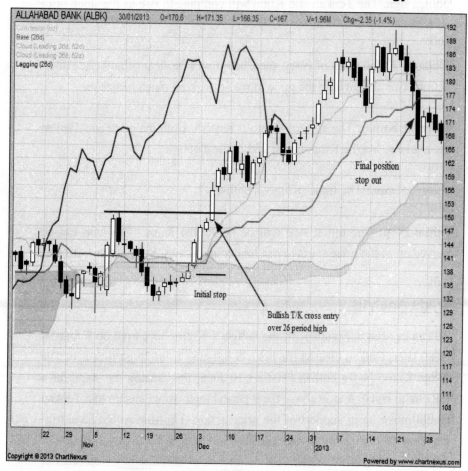

Figure 5.22: **Going long in Allahabad Bank — the bullish T/K cross and the initial stop are indicated on the chart**

Trade Set-up for Long Entry on 5 December

Tenkan / Kijun: Price is above the Tenkan and Kijun, which is a bullish sign. Tenkan is above the Kijun, which is also bullish. In Figure 5.22, the T/K cross occurred within the Kumo, which is considered a neutral signal. The Tenkan and Kijun will continue to rise as the stock price goes up.

Chikou: At the point of entry, the Chikou will be clear of any price interaction. This should help the price move up without much resistance.

Current Kumo: The current Kumo is bullish and the price, the Tenkan and the Kijun are above the cloud.

Future Kumo: The future Kumo is bullish.

Initial Stop: The initial stop will be below the Kijun. This stop can be moved up as the price starts to move higher and draw the Kijun up with it.

Trade Analysis

The bullish T/K cross occurred on 4 December (*see* Figure 5.22). All the Ichimoku components were lined up for a long entry at this point. The trader has to decide whether to get in on the 9-period high or the 26-period high. As the difference is minimal, it would make sense to place the buy stop above the 26-period high. This would ensure that the Tenkan and Kijun move up to support the price.

The initial stop would then be trailed as the stock price moves up and draws the Kijun with it. Profits should be taken along the way and the final position stopped out as price falters and closes below the Kijun.

~

With all the examples we have gone over in detail, the T/K cross strategy should be clear to the readers. There is no substitute for chart analysis on your own. Now that you are aware of the rules of this strategy, I would recommend visually observing as many charts as possible to determine entry and exit situations. It might take a little time and effort initially, but will get much easier as you get used to the analysis. And that will lead to profits.

6

How to Trade Any Asset in Any Market Using the Ichimoku

Ichimoku system can be used for trading any asset on any time frame. As trading becomes globalized, it is not uncommon for traders to trade different asset classes from all over the world. Some might be doing this for diversification, while others do so to take advantage of good chart set-up opportunities. No matter what the market is, the Ichimoku trading principles remain the same.

Imagine a scenario for a trader in India waiting for the stocks to get out of consolidation. Why should his portfolio sit idle while waiting for a trade set-up in stocks. Why not trade gold or silver futures if their charts are set-up for a Kumo break strategy or a T/K cross strategy? Maybe a particular currency pair is showing a breakout possibility. With the knowledge and practice of Ichimoku chart analysis, nothing should hold you back from trading any asset. Keep in mind that the dominant forces at the very heart of any trading strategy are always fear and greed. These two emotions are universal. Most traders will panic sell at the bottom and buy exuberantly at the top, be it in India or in the US. Hopefully, the

Ichimoku system will help you make trading decisions based on what you see on the chart and not what your emotions dictate.

In this chapter, we will consider of trading different securities in different countries, demonstrating how you can make money using the Ichimoku system trading any security, anywhere.

(Note: All prices in this chapter are in US Dollars)

Example 6.1: Going Long in Gold Futures Using the T/K Cross Strategy

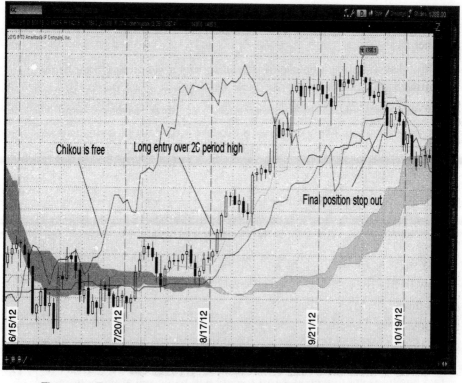

Figure 6.1: **Bullish trade in gold futures — the bullish T/K cross and the entry points are indicated on the chart**

Trade Set-up for Long Entry on 21 August

Tenkan / Kijun: In the chart of gold futures in Figure 6.1, the price is above both Tenkan and Kijun, which is a bullish signal. Tenkan is above the Kijun, which is also bullish. Also, the Tenkan and Kijun will continue to rise as the stock price goes up, thus offering support to the gold futures.

Chikou: At the point of entry, the Chikou will be clear of any price interaction. This should help the price move up without encountering much resistance.

Current Kumo: The current Kumo is bullish.

Future Kumo: The future Kumo is also bullish, thus confirming all the other indicators.

Initial Stop: The initial stop will be below the Kijun. This stop can be moved up as the price starts to move higher and draws the Kijun up with it.

Trade Analysis

The initial bullish T/K cross in gold futures occurred on 25 July (*see* Figure 6.1). However, note that the Chikou was then below the price from 26 days ago. It broke free only with the candle of 27 July. Traders could set a buy order above the high of this candle as all Ichimoku components were now lined up for a bullish trade. Prices then wavered along, taking support on the Kijun before finally picking up steam. Notice that when the order would have triggered, one was actually buying above the 26-period high and not the 9-period high. It's just a small premium to pay for getting the Kijun on your side!

Partial profits should continuously be taken as the price moves up and finally the entire remaining position should be stopped out on 15 October as the Kijun was breached.

Example 6.2: Selling Silver Futures Short Using the T/K Cross Strategy

Figure 6.2: **Selling silver futures short — the bearish T/K cross and trade entry point are indicated on the chart**

Trade Set-up for Short Entry on 19 February

Tenkan / Kijun: In the chart in Figure 6.2, the price is below both Tenkan and Kijun, which is a bearish sign. Tenkan is below the Kijun, which is also bearish. Both Tenkan and Kijun will continue to fall as the price goes lower, offering resistance to the futures.

Chikou: At the point of entry, the Chikou will be clear of any price inter-action. This should help the price move down without much support com-ing in.

Current Kumo: The current Kumo is bearish.

Future Kumo: The future Kumo is also bearish, thus confirming all the other indicators. Notice that this section is strongly trending down as Senkou A and Senkou B are both being drawn down.

Initial Stop: The initial stop will be placed above the Kijun. This stop can be moved down as the price starts to move lower and draws the Kijun down with it.

Trade Analysis

In the chart in Figure 6.2, the initial bearish T/K cross occurred on 13 Feb-ruary. All Ichimoku components, except the Chikou, were then lined up for a short entry. This happened on 15 February. A sell entry order should be placed below the low of this candle, which is the 9- as well as the 26-period low.

Partial profits should continuously be taken as the price moves down and the entire remaining position should be stopped out once the price closes below the Kijun.

Example 6.3: Bullish Intraday Trade in Oil Futures Using Kumo Break Strategy

Figure 6.3: **Long Intraday trade in oil futures — the bullish Kumo break and long entry point are indicated**

Trade Set-up for Long Entry at 11.15 a.m. on 30 May

Tenkan / Kijun: As you can see in the 5-minute chart of oil futures in Figure 6.3, on 30 May the price is above the Tenkan and Kijun, this is a bullish sign. Tenkan is above the Kijun, which is also bullish. Both Tenkan and Kijun will continue to rise as the price of oil futures goes up offering support to the price.

Chikou: At the point of entry, the Chikou will be clear of any price interaction. This should help the price move up without encountering much resistance.

Current Kumo: The current Kumo is bearish and extremely thin.

Future Kumo: The future Kumo is also bullish, thus confirming all the other indicators.

Initial Stop: The initial stop will be below the Kijun. This stop can be moved up as prices start to move higher and draw the Kijun up.

Trade Analysis

This example shows Ichimoku on a 5-minute chart of oil futures (Figure 6.3). A bullish Kumo break occurs at the close of the 11.00 a.m. 5-minute candle. Notice that the Chikou was facing resistance at this time from the candle of 26 (5-min) periods ago. One can visually analyze at this point that the Chikou will be free of price congestion on the next candle. A buy order above the candle would be the correct entry strategy for this Kumo break. This trade would have resulted in about a $1 move in less than half an hour.

Partial profits should be taken as the price moves up and finally the entire remaining position should be stopped out below the Kijun.

Example 6.4: Long Trade in the Currency Pairs Using Kumo Break Strategy

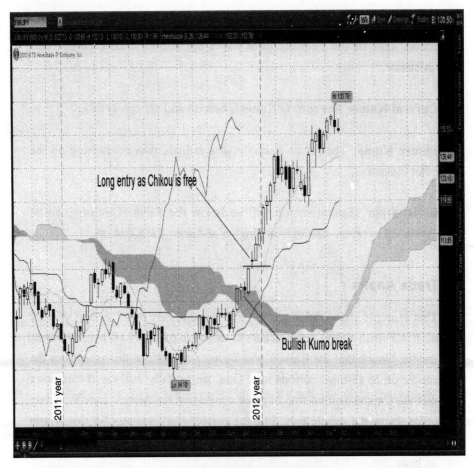

Figure 6.4: **Weekly chart for long trade in currency pairs — note the entry and bullish Kumo break points**

Trade Set-up for Long Entry in the Week of 17 December

Tenkan / Kijun: As you would note in the weekly chart in Figure 6.4, the price on 17 December is above both Tenkan and Kijun which is a bullish sign. Tenkan is above the Kijun, which is also bullish. Both Tenkan and Kijun will continue to rise as the price goes up, offering it support.

Chikou: At the point of entry, the Chikou will be clear of any price interaction. This should help the price moving up without much resistance coming in.

Current Kumo: Price is above current Kumo.

Future Kumo: The future Kumo is bullish, confirming all the other indicators.

Initial Stop: The initial stop will be below the Kijun. This stop can be raised as the price starts to move higher and draws the Kijun up with it.

Trade Analysis

Figure 6.4 shows a weekly chart for the Euro / Yen currency pair. You would notice that the bullish Kumo break occurred the week of November 26. However, the future Kumo was still bearish at this point. The Chikou was free of price congestion from 26 weeks ago. In the next couple of weeks, the future Senkou A crossed Senkou B to give the bullish Kumo twist. Keep in mind that since this is a weekly chart, trades will last much longer and could potentially yield huge profits like in this case.

Partial profits should be taken along the way as the price moves up and the final remaining position should be stopped out below the Kijun.

Example 6.5: Long and Short Trades in Australian Dollar Futures Using the Kumo Break Strategy

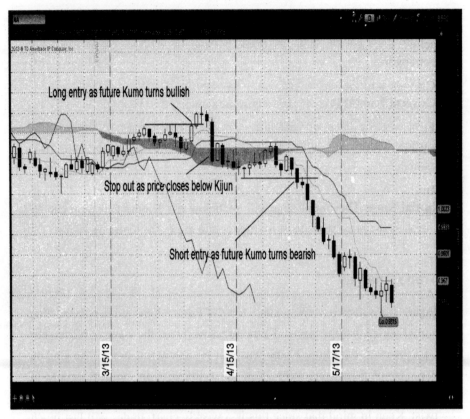

Figure 6.5: **Buying long — and short selling — Australian dollar futures — the Kumo breaks and entry points are indicated on the chart**

In this case, we will look at two possible trades using the Ichimoku system.

Trade Set-up for Long Entry on 9 April

Tenkan / Kijun: For the long entry, the price is above the Tenkan and Kijun, which is a bullish sign. Tenkan is above the Kijun, which is also bullish. Moreover, both Tenkan and Kijun will continue to rise as the futures price goes up, thus offering support to the price.

Chikou: At the point of entry, the Chikou will be clear of any price interaction.

Current Kumo: The current Kumo is bearish.

Future Kumo: The future Kumo is bullish, confirming all the other indicators.

Initial Stop: The initial stop will be below the Kijun. This stop can be moved up as the price starts to move higher and draw the Kijun up.

Trade Analysis

As can be seen in the chart in Figure 6.5, a bullish T/K cross occurred in the Australian Dollar futures on 15 March. However, the Chikou was then below price from 26 days ago. After a couple of weeks, the futures price closed above the Kumo. Notice how the price pulled back to the flat Kumo, finding support on the Tenkan and the bottom of the Kumo itself. On 5 April, the future Kumo turned bullish setting up for a long entry above the 9-period high as highlighted on the chart, which was also the 26-period high. This ensured that both Tenkan and Kijun would be pulled up upon trade execution.

The trade would have resulted in a small loss as price fe'l through the Kijun four days later. Remember, keep the losses small and let the profits run.

Trade Set-Up for Short Entry on 7 May

Tenkan / Kijun: As can be seen in the chart in Figure 6.5, the price is below the Tenkan and Kijun, which is a bearish sign. Tenkan is below the Kijun, which is also bearish. The Tenkan and Kijun will both continue to fall as the price heads lower, offering resistance to the stock.

Chikou: At the point of entry, the Chikou will be clear of any price interaction.

Current Kumo: The current Kumo is bearish.

Future Kumo: The future Kumo is also bearish, confirming all the other indicators.

Initial Stop: The initial stop will be above the Kijun. This stop can be moved down as the price starts to move lower and draws the Kijun down with it

Trade Analysis

Price closed below the Kumo on 23 April. At this time, however, the future Kumo was still bullish. On 29 April, Senkou A crossed below Senkou B to form the bearish Kumo twist. Placing a sell order below the 9-period low would ensure that the Chikou would be in open territory. The sell order point is indicated on the chart in Figure 6.5.

Profits should be taken as the price moves down and the final remaining position should be stopped out when price closes below the Kijun.

Example 6.6: Going Long in Citibank Using the Kumo Break Strategy

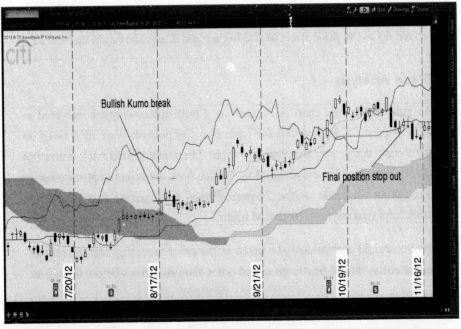

Bullish Kumo break

Final position stop out

Figure 6.6: **Going long in Citibank on NYSE — the bullish Kumo break and the final stop out are highlighted on the chart**

Trade Set-up for Long Entry on 21 August

Tenkan / Kijun: In Figure 6.6, the price is above both Tenkan and Kijun, which is bullish. Tenkan is above the Kijun, which is also bullish. The Tenkan and Kijun will both continue to rise as the stock goes up, offering support to the stock.

Chikou: At the point of entry, the Chikou will be clear of any price interaction.

Current Kumo: The current Kumo is bearish.

Future Kumo: The future Kumo is bullish, thus confirming all the other indicators.

Initial Stop: The initial stop will be below the Kijun. This stop can be moved up as the price starts to rise higher and draws the Kijun up with it.

Trade Analysis

As indicated on the chart in Figure 6.6, a bullish Kumo break occurred in Citigroup on 20 August. All the Ichimoku components were then lined up for a long entry over the 9-period high. The stock pulled back some but reversed soon as buyers stepped in. Notice how the Kijun kept moving up throughout the trade as the 26-period lows kept getting higher and the stock kept making new 26-period highs.

Profits should continuously be taken as the price moves up and the remaining position should finally be exited when the price gives below the Kijun.

Example 6.7: Shorting 10-year US Treasury Notes

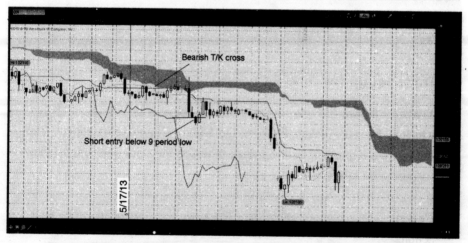

Figure 6.7: **10-year US Treasury notes provide shorting opportunity on 4-hour chart — the bearish T/K cross and the short entry point are indicated on the chart**

Trade Set-Up for Short Entry on 22 May

Tenkan / Kijun: In Figure 6.7, the price is below both Tenkan and Kijun, which is a bearish sign. Tenkan is below the Kijun, which is also bearish. Also, both Tenkan and Kijun will continue to fall as the price heads lower, thus offering resistance to the price.

Chikou: At the point of entry, the Chikou will be clear of any price interaction.

Current Kumo: The current Kumo is bearish.

Future Kumo: The future Kumo is also bearish, confirming all the other indicators.

Initial Stop: The initial stop should be placed above the Kijun. This stop can be moved down as the price starts to move lower and draws the Kijun down with it.

Trade Analysis

Figure 6.7 shows a 4-hour timeframe chart for the 10-year US Treasury Notes. You can see the strong bearish T/K cross that happened with the 5.00 p.m. candle on 20 May. At this point, the Chikou was still in the price congestion from 26 periods ago. It broke free to the downside with the 9.00 a.m. candle on 22 May. Setting a sell order below the low of this candle would have triggered the trade on the 5.00 p.m. candle on the same day. The price rallied back up but failed to close above the Kijun. Notice how many candles bumped against the flat Kijun and were rejected.

Profits should continuously be taken as the price moves down and the final remaining position be stopped out when the price closes below the Kijun.

7

Ichimoku Trading Tips

Avoid Entering a Trade Before Earnings Announcements

Fundamental news, such as an earnings announcement, can render technical analysis irrelevant. Investor sentiment can change overnight from bullish to extreme bearish, or from bearish to overly bullish. This does not bode well for someone using charts to make trading decisions. The bullishness of a chart can be instantly negated as price succumbs to investor fear and greed in a moment of panic or euphoria, respectively. The consequences can be disastrous for the portfolio if the price gaps heavily against you. There could also be an occasional surprise announcement which will have the same effect. However, those are the unknowns a trader has to face. Earnings announcements, on the other hand, are known well in advance. The trader can liquidate the position a day before such an earnings announcement and use the capital for another high probability trade. To illustrate, and to emphasize, this point look at the chart of Infosys Ltd. in Figure 7.1.

Figure 7.1: **The chart of Infosys shows how fundamental news can negate a good trade set-up**

No technical system can withstand a fundamental shock. So, it's best to avoid trading in stocks with known upcoming fundamental events.

Avoid Trading Low Volume Stocks

The main reason why technical analysis works is because markets (traders) have memory. The greater the number of traders in a stock, the stronger the memory. And a strong memory contributes to better repeatability of patterns. Even in Western technical analysis, memory is what makes patterns, such as the double bottom or ascending / descending triangles, work. Recall the use of Chikou in our case. Why do we need to see the Chikou clear of price congestion? (Refer to Chapter 2 for explanation.)

It stands to reason that having low trading volume means less memory. This means when you expect the price to behave in a certain way at key levels, there is good chance it will not. As a technical trader, this is not what you want. Repeatability is crucial in trading. If I expect the price to find support on a flat Kijun in a trend, the price needs to do just that. If the price is all over the place disregarding the Kijun, trading will be more of gambling. As the chart in Figure 7.2 highlights, low volume charts are notorious for such behavior.

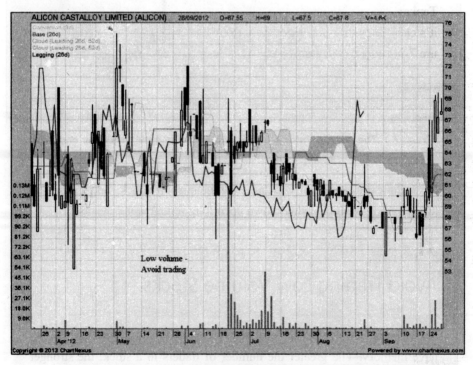

Figure 7.2: **The haphazard movement of price in the chart of Alicon Castalloy Ltd. shows why you should avoid trades based on low volume charts**

Timing Entries After Pullbacks in a Trend

Traders can enter a trending stock even after they miss, say, the initial T/K cross or the Kumo breakout entry. We know that prices use the Tenkan and Kijun as support in a bullish trend. Conversely, prices use the Tenkan and Kijun as resistance in a downtrend. A strategy can be formed using this knowledge.

Strategy in a Bullish Trend

Wait for a pullback of the stock below the Tenkan. It will probably test the Kijun for support. If it finds support, there is a good chance of the price continuing in the uptrend. If this happens, and price closes back above the Tenkan, place a buy order above the 9-period high — the 26-period high if it's close enough to the 9-period high — with a stop below the Kijun. Figure 7.3 shows this strategy in action.

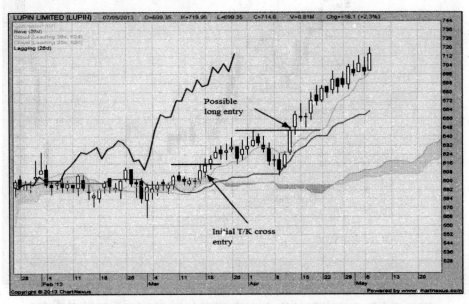

Figure 7.3: **How to jump into an uptrend even after missing the initial set-up by using a pullback**

Strategy in a Bearish Trend

Wait for a pullback of the stock above the Tenkan. In many cases, the price will test the Kijun for resistance. If the supply is strong, the price will fall back and continue its downtrend. When price closes back below the Tenkan, place a sell order below the 9-period low — the 26-period low if both are close enough. The stop loss should be placed above the Kijun and trailed with it as it moves down with price. You can notice in the chart of Tata Steel in Figure 7.4 that one had two occasions to enter a short trade after missing the initial Kumo breakout trade.

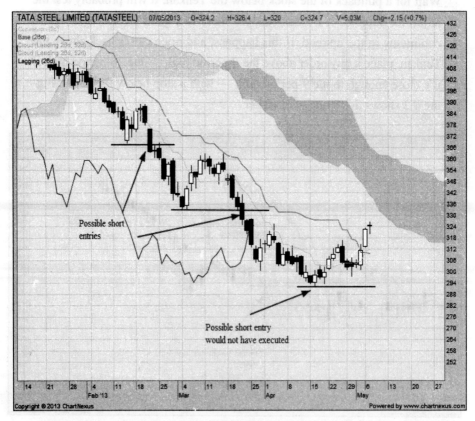

Figure 7.4: **Two possible entry opportunities to go short in Tata Steel during pullbacks**

The chart of Reliance Infrastructure in Figure 7.5 provides traders with two short entry possibilities after the initial Kumo break strategy. Keep in mind, however, that there will be instances where one enters the trade and the trend reverses. Having a stop loss in place assures, in most instances, that the loss will be minimal.

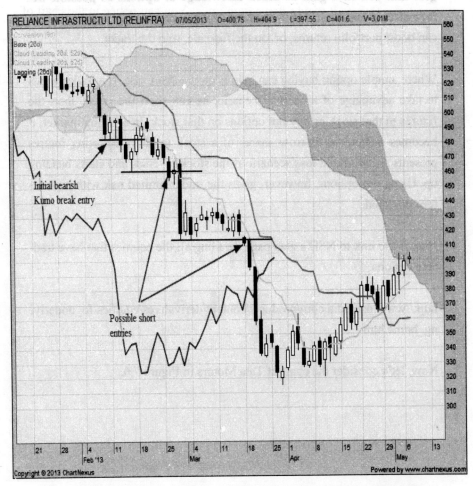

Figure 7.5: Reliance Infrastructure provides good short entries during pullbacks even after the initial bearish Kumo break set-up

Option Trading Strategies with the Ichimoku System

Option (a derivative) trading is a world of its own. **This section assumes that the reader is familiar with options. If not, I would strongly suggest that you first gain as much knowledge of options as possible before attempting their use in trading.** Options provide big leverage which can boost portfolio returns; or, on the flip side, ruin the trader.

Where simple option buying can help is on the short side. If a trader wants to take advantage of a bearish scenario, he can short the stock, short the futures in that stock or buy put options on that stock. In a falling market, it becomes difficult to borrow shares of a stock to short. Shorting futures presents an unlimited loss scenario if the stock reverses and starts heading up. Using put options, however, gives the trader limited risk with high return potential.

Here is the link to NSE's web page detailing all the equities that have tradable options.

http://www.nseindia.com/products/content/derivatives/equities/fo_underlyi ng_home.htm

Now, let's consider the chart of Tata Motors in Figure 7.6.

Figure 7.6: **Buying put options for short trading Tata Motors using the Kumo break strategy**

The idea would be to buy a put option when one of the Ichimoku strategies calls for a short entry. A deep in-the-money (ITM) Put option can mimic the movement of the underlying stock. In this case, one could have bought the June 270 Put option as the stock broke through the 9-period low. This ITM Put option would have increased in value as the stock moved down. Profit-taking rules remain the same. Profits should be taken on a continuous basis and the entire position should be exited when the price trades, or closes, above the Kijun.

Trading in the Direction of the Bigger Trend

'The trend is your friend' is a well known and powerful adage in financial markets. There is a good reason for it. Markets are based on human psychology. Once the investor sentiment establishes in a certain way, whether bullish or bearish, it takes time for it to change. In bullish trending markets, every dip is used as an opportunity to enter long positions. In strong bear markets, on the other hand, every rally is sold into. Doing the reverse could wipe out one's portfolio in a hurry.

So how do you find the prevailing trend? To do that, look at the higher time frame Ichimoku chart.

Say, for example, one is looking to swing trade using daily time frame charts. The idea, then would be to look at the weekly chart for direction.

- If price is above the Kumo cloud on the weekly chart, then only bullish trades should be taken on the daily chart.

- Conversely, if price is below the Kumo cloud on the weekly chart, then take only bearish trades on the daily chart.

Let's now consider the chart of Indusind Bank in Figure 7.7.

As you would note, there are two bearish Kumo break signals in March. Both the signals satisfy our Kumo break strategy for a short entry. In both cases, price was below the Tenkan, which was below the Kijun. The future Kumo was bearish and the Chikou was free. Both the trades would have lost money. Again, nothing wrong with having a losing trade. But, as we will see with the chart in Figure 7.8, this could be avoided.

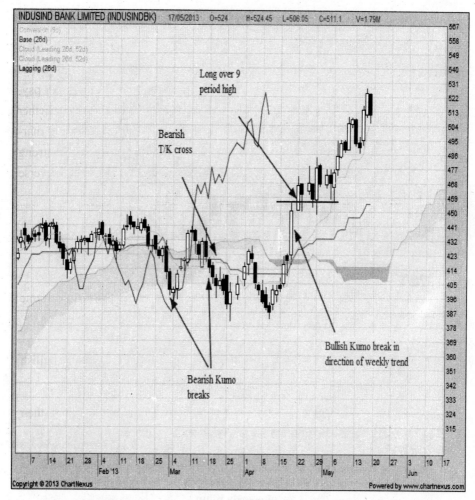

INDUSIND BANK LIMITED (INDUSINDBK)   17/05/2013   O=524   H=524.45   L=506.05   C=511.1   V=1.79M

Conversion (9d)
Base (26d)
Cloud (Leading 26d, 52d)
Cloud (Leading 26d, 52d)
Lagging (26d)

Long over 9
period high

Bearish
T/K cross

Bullish Kumo break in
direction of weekly trend

Bearish Kumo
breaks

Copyright © 2013 ChartNexus   Powered by www.chartnexus.com

Figure 7.7: **Daily chart of Indusind Bank indicating futures for short trades**

Next, notice the bearish T/K cross. Our strategy criteria for a short entry was met in this case. The trade would also have resulted in a loss. But now look at the bullish trade that should have been initiated on the Kumo break to the upside. This would have resulted in a nice rally for the trader. To see

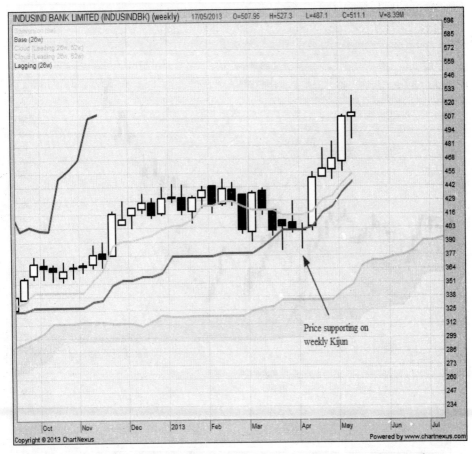

Figure 7.8: **Weekly chart of Indusind Bank clearly negates any short trades as the price was above the Kumo and also very close to the major support of weekly Kijun**

why the first three trades failed and the fourth succeeded, look at the weekly chart of the stock shown in Figure 7.8.

The chart is self-explanatory. There was no reason to take the short trades in this stock as not only was the price above the Kumo, but also very close to the major support of weekly Kijun. The bullish trade, however, was aligned with the bigger trend to the upside.

As another example, let's consider the daily chart of Indian Overseas Bank (IOB) in Figure 7.9. Indian Overseas Bank closed decisively above the Kumo on 30 December 2014. On 1 January, the continued up move also pulled the Tenkan above the Kijun. At this point, the future Kumo was bullish and Chikou was above the price indicating good upside momentum in the stock.

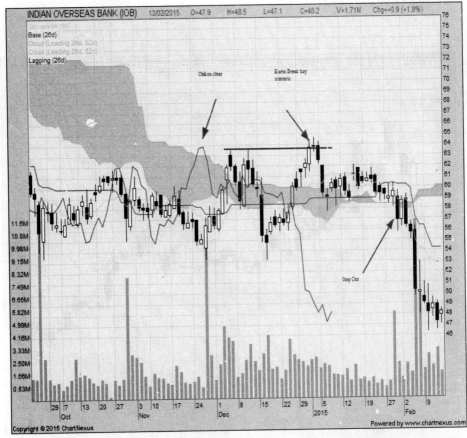

Figure 7.9: **Daily chart of Indian Overseas Bank suggesting long entry trades**

All conditions were satisfied for entering a long position using the Kumo break strategy. Things however did not work out for the trade and it had to be closed for a loss on 30 January as it closed below the Kumo.

Could this losing trade have been avoided? To answer this question with relative ease, look at the chart in Figure 7.10. This is a weekly chart of Indian Overseas Bank.

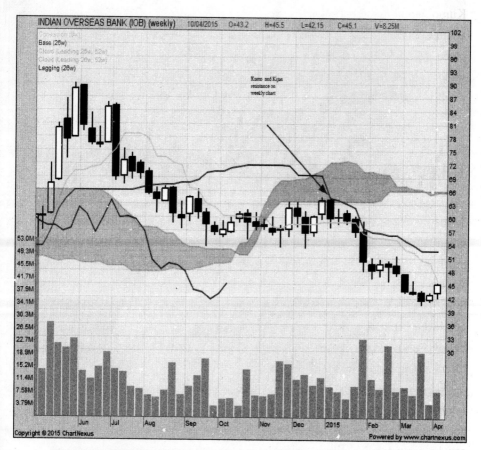

Figure 7.10: **Weekly chart of Indian Overseas Bank clearly shows strong resistance by the Kumo and the Kijun highlighting the futility of going long**

The weekly chart clearly shows strong resistance to the stock in terms of the Kumo and the Kijun. Where the daily chart showed a buy scenario, the weekly chart showed otherwise. Why enter positions when there is a conflict between the smaller and the higher time frame chart?

Having said that, there will be times when trading the bullish side on the daily chart while the weekly chart is bearish might lead to profitable trades. An example would be a stock trading below, or within, the Kumo, but above the Tenkan and Kijun on the weekly chart. If you notice a Kumo break on the daily chart, the trade can then be taken with stops in place. Just keep in mind that it will not be a high probability trade. The same would be true for a bearish trade based on the daily chart, when the weekly chart is bullish.

Take Partial Profits as They Accumulate

Throughout the book I have recommended that partial profits should be taken as the position moves in the desired direction and starts becoming profitable. One can employ a variety of profit taking strategies based on Western technical indicators like Fibonnaci retracements or pivot points. Some traders like to take profits at pre-determined price levels or percentage levels. Others will ride the original position until they are stopped out below / above a key moving average support. Ichimoku trading system offers a unique stop loss and profit-taking setup.

Ichimoku being a trend following system, the Tenkan and Kijun typically act as guides for the stock's price in the trending direction. The Tenkan can be considered a minor support level and the Kijun a major support level in case of a bullish trend. Correspondingly, the Tenkan acts as a minor resistance level and the Kijun acts as a major resistance level for down trending stocks. This trait can be used to form a system for placing stops.

We have already discussed using the Kijun as our initial stop loss point. Once a trade is initiated with a Kumo break or a T/K cross strategy, the price should not be violating the support (or resistance for a bearish trade) offered by the Kijun. As the price starts moving in the expected direction, the Kijun will begin trending with it. The initial stop can be moved up (or down for bearish trade) with the Kijun.

Profit-Taking Strategy for Bullish Trending Markets

Divide your trading position in three parts. Take one part off once the price closes below the Tenkan. At this point there are two things that can happen. Either the price keeps going down and closes below the Kijun, or the price reverses and closes back above the Tenkan, thus continuing its uptrend. In the first case, close out the remaining two parts of your position. In the second case, continue to hold the two parts until the next time the price closes below the Tenkan. At that point, you should take profits on one more part. Now you are left with just one part of the original position, which should be closed / stopped out below the Kijun.

Let's consider the chart of Syndicate Bank in Figure 7.11.

Assume 300 shares were purchased at about ₹ 109 on 27 September following a bullish Kumo break. Using our exit strategy, 100 shares should be sold on 26 October for about ₹ 118.50. The remaining 200 shares should be liquidated on 16 November for about ₹ 119.

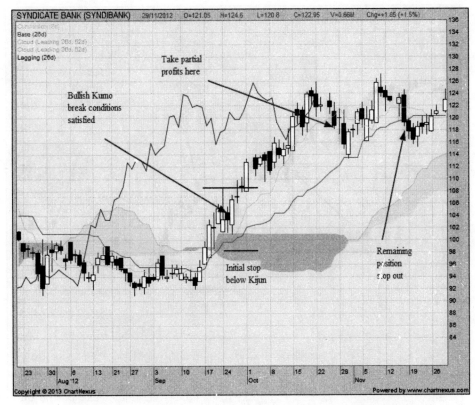

Figure 7.11: **Using the Tenkan for taking profits in a bullish trend**

Profit-Taking Strategy for Bearish Trending Markets

Again, divide the position in three parts. Take one part off as the price closes above the Tenkan. At this point there are two things that can happen. Either the price keeps going up and closes above the Kijun, or the price reverses and closes back below the Tenkan, thus continuing its downtrend. In the first case, close out the remaining two parts of the position. In the second case, continue to hold the two parts until the next time the price closes above the Tenkan. At that point, take profits on one more part. Now you are left with just one part, namely one-third of the original position, which should be closed / stopped out above the Kijun.

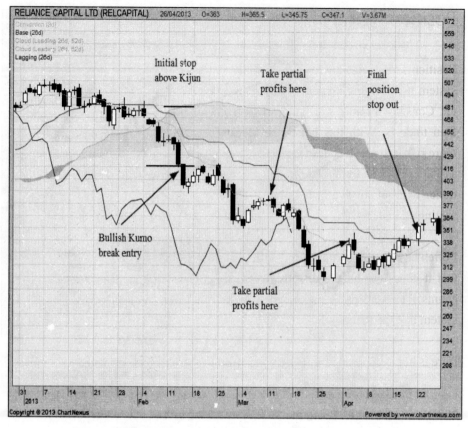

Figure 7.12: **Using the Kijun to take profits in Reliance Capital**

Let's consider the profit taking strategy in the case of Reliance Capital whose chart is shown in Figure 7.12.

Assume 3 Put options were bought on 14 February on Reliance Capital with the stock trading at 415. On 11 March, the stock closed above the Tenkan at 382. This would be the trigger to close out 1 Put option. The stock then reversed and continued its downtrend. On 2 April, the price once again closed above the Tenkan at 335. This would be a trigger for liquidating another Put option. The remaining Put option would be closed on 22 April as the price closed above the Kijun at 355.

Position Sizing

Position sizing your trades is as critical to trading success as the trading system itself. Using random position sizes for trades is a recipe for disaster. Consider a trader who judges that trade A has better reward potential than trade B. With this belief, he invests more capital, taking on much more risk in trade A than in trade B. If trade A goes south and trade B does as expected, the trader might still be sitting on big overall losses. The trader will not survive in his trading career for long with this way of investing capital.

I often talk about position sizing in terms of maximum risk. Keep in mind that it is easy to handle profits. Not so for losses. So a strategy that accounts for fixed losses makes good sense for a high probability trading system like the Ichimoku.

Here is how you would implement the fixed loss position sizing strategy:

Scenario 1:

- Portfolio = ₹ 10 lakh

- Maximum risk % per position = 0.2 %

- Maximum risk for any position = 0.2 % x 10 lakh = ₹ 2,000

- Strategy = Bullish T/K cross

- Stock price = ₹ 100

- 9-period high = ₹ 101

- Entry point = ₹ 101.50

- Current Kijun price = ₹ 98

- Stop loss setting = ₹ 97.5

- Maximum loss = 101.5 – 97.5 = ₹ 4

- Total number of shares to be bought = Max risk tolerance / Maximum loss = 2,000/4 = 500

- Total capital for this position = 500 x 101.5 = ₹ 50,750.

Scenario 2:

- Portfolio = ₹ 10 lakh

- Maximum risk % per position = 0.2 %

- Maximum risk for any position = 0.2 % x 10 lakh = ₹ 2,000

- Strategy = Bullish T/K cross

- Stock price = ₹ 100

- 9-period high = ₹ 101

- Entry point = ₹ 101.5

- Current Kijun price = ₹ 96

- Stop loss setting = ₹ 95.5

- Maximum loss = 101.5 – 95.5 = ₹ 6

- Total number of shares to be bought = Max risk tolerance / Maximum loss = 2,000 ÷ 6 = 333

- Total capital for this position = 333 x 101.5 = ₹ 33,800.

Scenario 3:

- Portfolio = ₹ 10 lakh

- Maximum risk % per position = 0.2 %

- Maximum risk for any position = 0.2 % x 10 lakh = ₹ 2,000

- Strategy = Kumo Breakout

- Stock price = ₹ 100

- 9-period high = ₹ 101

- Entry point = ₹ 101.5

- Bottom of Kumo = ₹ 93

- Stop loss setting = ₹ 92.5

- Maximum loss = 101.5 – 92.5 = ₹ 9

- Total number of shares to be bought = Max risk tolerance / Maximum loss = 2,000 ÷ 9 = 222

- Total capital for this position = 222 x 101.5 = ₹ 22,533.

The three scenarios show how the quantity of shares bought changes with respect to the initial stop loss. If all the trades fail, the trader's maximum loss is capped at ₹ 2,000 each. Remember that if the Ichimoku strategy works and the stock goes in the direction as expected, the Kijun will move with it. The stop loss setting should be moved with the Kijun. So the maximum loss should only happen at the beginning of the trade. This, of course, assumes that some unexpected fundamental event does not gap the stock down beyond the stop setting.

This strategy allows the trader to be calm and confident when entering the trade as the maximum loss is both pre-defined and is one that the trader is comfortable with.

8

Conclusion

This is where the rubber meets the road. Knowing a system and using it in the proper context are two different things. There are plenty of traders who know ten different systems, but cannot implement even a single one. That's because they lack the confidence in their ability to actually profit from those systems. Keep in mind that the system is only a part of the trading equation. The trader's psychology is equally important. It is completely possible for two traders to take the exact same system and come out on two opposite ends of the profit scale. Why the difference? The personality of the traders!

What Type of Trading is Right for You?

It would be worthwhile to address this question before you start trading. Here are three different ways to profit from the market and the basic personality traits suitable for each. Analyze where you fit in!

Day Trading

This is where you open and close positions during the day. The assets are not held overnight. You are using larger position sizes to make quick, small, multiple gains.

A day trader typically has the following personality traits:

- You are uncomfortable with the risk of holding assets overnight because fundamental news coming out after hours could disrupt your strategy.

- You are a quick thinker and decision maker.

- You have strong emotional control. This is extremely important as your emotions will be tested each and every minute you are in the trade.

Swing Trading

This is where you hold positions from a few days to a couple of weeks depending on the trend of the asset.

A swing trader typically has the following personality traits:

- You are comfortable with the risk of holding assets overnight. Your strategy takes into account any fundamental disruptions occurring after hours.

- You like to make entry / exit decisions in a relaxed state of mind. You might be working at a full-time job and need to make your call when you come home at night.

- You cannot handle the constant emotional ride during the day.

Long-term Trading (Investing)

This is where you hold positions for weeks to months at a time, typically using weekly charts.

Long term traders and investors usually have the following personality traits:

- You believe in the underlying fundamentals of the company you are investing in and are willing to give it more time to prove itself.

- You do not care about the day-to-day ups and downs of the market.

- Your ideal scenario is when an undervalued company exhibits good entry point on weekly charts.

So where do you fit in?

Once you have truthfully answered this question, you can proceed to choosing a strategy and making it your own. Keep in mind that losing trades will be a part of the game no matter what the style of trading is. Learn to handle them emotionally, and profitable trades will follow. Also, the market will throw one opportunity after the other at you. If you miss one, do not feel disappointed. There will be another one again tomorrow. Always keep your enthusiasm high and maintain a healthy positive expectancy of success.

Good luck — and happy wealth building.